D0419108

# Gardening under cover

# Gardening under cover

## Alan Titchmarsh

Illustrations by the Hayward Art Group
and Tony Streek

**Hamlyn**
London · New York · Sydney · Toronto

# Contents

First published in 1979 by
The Hamlyn Publishing Group Limited
London · New York · Sydney · Toronto
Astronaut House, Feltham, Middlesex

Filmset in England by Photocomp Ltd., Birmingham in 9 on 10pt
Monophoto Rockwell Light
Printed in Italy.

ISBN 0 600 34078 3

# Introduction

Once you've grappled with a patch of land and coaxed it into producing flowers, fruits and vegetables the chances are that it won't be long before you're eager to find ways of increasing and prolonging your harvest.

The most obvious way of doing this is to cultivate more ground, but space may not be available, and time to keep it in shape may be short too. Some kind of protective structure is the answer, for under a covering of glass or plastic even a small patch of land can be made to produce crops all the year round.

A row of cloches will bring you succulent early strawberries and a continuous supply of winter lettuce, and a frame will act as a store-house and nursery for many tender plants.

If you find yourself gazing miserably across a soggy garden on rainy days, invest in a greenhouse and potter away to your heart's content regardless of rain and snow.

In this book I've set out to show you what kind of structures are available – both simple and elaborate – and how they can best be used. There are cropping plans to keep your plot productive, and at the back of the book a list of manufacturers and suppliers who stock the equipment and sundries I've mentioned.

I've kept the instructions fairly basic; all too often gardening is made out to be a craft surrounded by mystique and riddled with pitfalls – in reality it relies heavily on common sense. Master a few basic principles and you'll find that gardening under cover is great fun.

*Alan Titchmarsh*

# Greenhouses

A flip through any gardening magazine or Sunday newspaper reveals that the range of greenhouses on the market now is remarkably extensive, making the matter of choosing one that much more difficult. The easiest way of whittling down this baffling selection to find just the one for you is to make a list of exactly what you and your plants will require.

**Good looks** There is no point in buying a greenhouse which has great scientific and technical merit if you can't stand the sight of it, so choose a structure that appeals to you.

**The right price** Cost is the other main consideration, though nowadays this need not be a great stumbling block, for well-designed polythene greenhouses are offered by manufacturers at prices to suit most people's pockets.

**What do you want to grow?** If pot plants are your interest, there is no point in buying a greenhouse glazed to ground level. One with half-timbered sides will suit you better, for it will hide from view watering cans and pots stored beneath the staging, and will also reduce heat loss. If you aim to be a prize tomato or chrysanthemum grower, then a glass-to-ground model is for you. However, if you want to keep your options open, choose a greenhouse which has a short timber wall right round or which has one side half-timbered and the other glazed to ground level.

**Light** Without a good supply of direct light, all plants become tall and spindly. Apart from ruining their appearance, this condition also saps their strength and lays them wide open to pest and disease attack.

Fortunately, most of today's greenhouses have a thin but strong framework and fairly large panes of glass (usually 60cm (2ft) square) which means that only a small amount of light is excluded.

**Air** As well as light, plants must have fresh air – not just the supply which was captured when the greenhouse was erected. In this stagnant atmosphere, damaging fungi and insects will thrive. Those plants which do not fall victim to pests and diseases may be burned up in the fierce heat generated by bright sunlight.

Ventilators are the answer, and most greenhouses are equipped with them in their ridges and sometimes along their sides. They are vital in both places for good air circulation which will promote healthy plant growth. Some polythene houses are not so well equipped, and only the doors at each end can be opened in the hope of causing a through-draught which may be assisted by a fan.

However, draughts in themselves are not a good thing and the greenhouse you choose should be well glazed, and the door a good fit, to keep out the chilling blasts of winter weather.

**Stability** Pinning the greenhouse securely to the ground is your responsibility, but when you buy a greenhouse, look for one which is sturdily made and well bolted and braced together on the inside. The stability of polythene houses depends even more on the way in which they are erected – if they are not firmly anchored you may well see them floating through the sky, and small tears in the sheeting will allow the wind to enter and rip them to pieces.

**Accessibility** Even if you are not unduly large, consider how easy it will be to get in and out of your new greenhouse. Many are fitted with quite narrow doorways and if you want to wheel in barrowloads of compost and gravel you may be faced with problems.

There are models with extra-wide or double doors which can make life much easier.

## Wood or aluminium?

The choice of structural material nowadays is usually confined to wood and aluminium alloy.

Most timber greenhouses are constructed from western red cedar, a North-American rot-resistant wood which, if treated with a protective water repellant every few years, will last a lifetime. Some cedar greenhouses are soaked in this preservative before being sold, others may have to be painted with it before they are erected. Other softwood greenhouses, which are usually made of Baltic pine, are cheaper than their cedar equivalents. The timber is not so durable as cedar and needs to be treated with preservative and coated with external quality paint if it is to wear well.

Aluminium alloy greenhouses have really swamped the market in recent years and are certainly the best for the lazy gardener as they need no maintenance, other than the oiling of moving parts and the routine cleaning of glass. The framework is strong, light and not at all bulky, and the use of glazing clips rather than the old-fashioned, but effective, putty makes them quick and easy to erect.

A certain amount of corrosion does take place when aluminium is first exposed to the weather, and this shows as a white powdery deposit. The process goes no further though. Some manufacturers are now offering aluminium greenhouses which have been coated with a white or green acrylic paint – an alternative if you like the properties of aluminium but not the appearance.

## Glass or plastic?

For cheapness, and safety where children are at large, plastic greenhouses (usually made of 600 gauge sheeting) are unbeatable, but they also have their drawbacks. Polythene and PVC collect dirt and will quickly break down in daylight until, after a couple of years, they have become brittle and yellow. Other more rigid plastics may last longer, but after six years or so even they will have to be renewed (although some plastics guaranteed for ten years are now coming on to the market – at a price).

Heat is lost very rapidly through plastic, especially if it is corrugated. This wastage allows greater temperature fluctuation and provides you with higher heating bills. Condensation can be a problem too, for it drips from the plastic instead of running down it. A solution called Sun Clear is helpful here; it can be sprayed on the inside of the greenhouse to disperse these water droplets.

Ventilation is often inadequate, especially in long tunnels, and, if not securely anchored, plastic greenhouses can be blown away.

Set against these difficulties, the ease with which they can be erected, and their mobility, does make them a good choice where a temporary structure is required for moving around the garden. It is a simple job to uproot a small polythene greenhouse and plant it in another part of your plot, or even to fold it up and store it after spring seedlings have been raised.

Glass has its own list of good and bad features: if broken it can be both costly and dangerous; it is inflexible and, once erected, a 'glasshouse' is impossible to move around. On the other hand, glass is clear and allows in more light than polythene if it is kept clean; it can be coated with shading compounds and later cleaned effectively.

Glass is also a much more effective insulator than plastic, and a glass structure therefore costs less to heat; ventilation can be easily achieved; and, perhaps the greatest advantage of all, unless it happens to be inadvertently broken, glass will last indefinitely.

# Greenhouses

Whatever type you choose, the well-constructed greenhouse, although it may cost you more at the outset, will be with you for a greater length of time than one which is cheaper but more flimsily made. Before finally making up your mind, go to a garden centre or manufacturer's show ground and take a close look inside and outside the greenhouses available. The next few pages show the kinds you are most likely to see.

## Span-roof, half-timbered

In span-roofed greenhouses the two sides of the roof are of equal size and slope down to the same level. This kind, with half-timbered or brick-built sides, is the best to buy if you are growing only pot plants – the wood or brick area cuts heat loss, and staging presents the plants at a convenient height.

Span-roof, half-timbered greenhouse

## Span-roof, glazed to the ground

Although it costs more to heat, a greenhouse glazed to ground level allows tomatoes and tall pot plants to be grown on beds of gravel or compost where they can make full use of all the light available without running out of headroom. If this kind of greenhouse is to be positioned on a lawn, surround it with flagstones to keep the mower at a safe distance. Models glazed to the ground on only one side are also available, giving you the opportunity to grow tomatoes *and* pot plants.

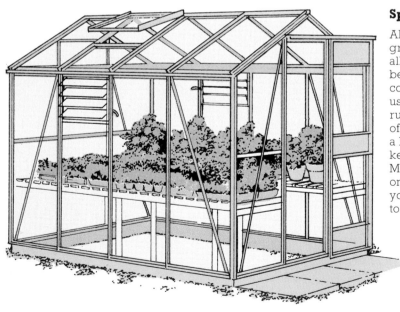

Span-roof, glazed-to-the-ground greenhouse

8

## Dutch type

Much used on nurseries, this type of greenhouse has large panes of glass (usually measuring about 1·5m by 75cm (5 by 2½ft)) and sloping sides. Light transmission is particularly good but breakages are expensive due to the size of the panes. The sloping sides make it impossible to position tall plants near the glass – unless, like cucumbers and vines, they can be trained on wires. Though originally made of timber, Dutch style houses are now also available in aluminium.

Dutch-type greenhouse

## Octagonal

A pleasing appearance and compact dimensions have made this design very popular. Light transmission and ventilation are both good, and a surprising number of plants can be accommodated on the shelves. The minimum of movement is necessary inside the greenhouse – a valuable asset to the disabled gardener who can swivel round and attend to plants easily from a wheelchair. If your garden is minute, this is the model for you.

Octagonal greenhouse

Uneven-span greenhouse

## Uneven span

In this type of structure the sides may be of different heights and the roof sections at different angles. Here only one roof panel is fitted and the entire house is 'glazed' with rigid corrugated plastic, though glass and aluminium, or glass and wood, models are also manufactured. Tall plants such as tomatoes can be grown on one side and pot plants supported by staging on the other. It is usually recommended that the largest side of the house faces south.

# Greenhouses

## Dome shaped

This roomy aluminium greenhouse will appeal to gardeners who like space-age designs. It is known technically as a geodetic dome and the glazing bars and triangular panes combine to make the house very strong. Several of the panes are hinged to allow ventilation, including the one over the door on this model, which also allows easier access for tall plants and people.

**Dome-shaped greenhouse**

## Miniature lean-to

Where space is limited to a patio or balcony, this type of greenhouse, in glass or plastic, will give pleasure without taking up too much room. Some kinds rest on the floor while others can be suspended on a wall, and either can be placed against a window. Being so small, these greenhouses are subject to rapid temperature fluctuation, so either site them on a north wall where the light is indirect, or use them only for sun-loving plants. They are ideal for raising plants from seeds and cuttings.

**Above** Lean-to greenhouse

**Below right** Miniature lean-to greenhouse

## Lean-to

Fitted to the side of the house, a lean-to can improve the insulation of your home and also make use of any escaping heat. It is also easy to extend the central heating system into it if plants which need warmth are being grown. Both glass-to-ground and half-timbered types are available. Painting the back wall white will improve the light intensity in any lean-to, and shelves can be fixed on the wall at intervals from floor to ceiling. Being close to the house, a lean-to will be especially appreciated in wet weather.

## Greenhouse and shed combined

The perfect solution for the gardener who wants everything in one place. The shed can be used for potting and as a tool store, and the lean-to greenhouse is right next door. With the outside door set in the shed half, the greenhouse temperature is unaffected by comings and goings. Span-roof greenhouses are also available with a shed attached to one end.

## Miniature free-standing

This little 'growing box' has all the advantages of a miniature lean-to plus the benefit of being mobile. Take out the plants and you can move it around your roof garden or patio any time you feel like a change. There are various designs to choose from – this one has a rigid plastic dome as a roof panel and sliding glass doors for ventilation.

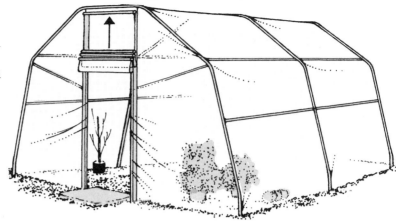

## Plastic tunnel

Cheapness and ease of erection are the chief advantages of this type of greenhouse. The tubular steel frame is easily put together and a one-piece polythene envelope fits over it. No foundations are necessary, for the ends of the polythene are buried in the ground for anchorage. Ventilation is controlled by means of the door panels at each end which move up and down on two strings, and the whole envelope can be removed and renewed when it wears out. The structure can be moved over crops growing in the open, and also used with staging to cultivate pot plants.

Plastic tunnel

Miniature free-standing greenhouse

## Plastic dome

Another 'geodetic' shape, this time in polythene. One of the large triangular facets folds back as a door and ventilation is achieved in the same way. The tubular aluminium frame is easily assembled and is staked to the ground for stability. Again, a replacement envelope can be bought when the original wears out.

Plastic dome

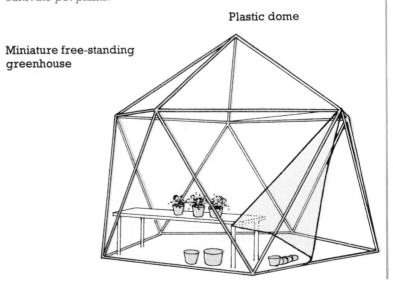

# Greenhouses

There are lots of do's and don'ts thrown at gardeners who are about to put up a greenhouse. Much of the advice is very sensible, but some of it can only be followed in gardens where space is plentiful. On small urban plots a compromise has to be made.

Firstly, check with your local authority to see if they require planning permission. A lean-to is likely to increase your rates, and a free-standing greenhouse may have to be sited a certain distance from any boundary fence.

If space does allow you to pick the perfect site for your greenhouse, these are the points to keep in mind:

**1 Light** Don't put up a greenhouse in a spot overshadowed by tall buildings. Keep away from trees too; as well as cutting out light they can move the foundations, foul the glass and harbour pests and diseases which may attack your greenhouse plants. If the branches are blown off in a wind you may not even have a greenhouse to worry about.

**2 Shelter** Avoid sites which are greatly exposed to wind. Apart from increasing the likelihood of the greenhouse being blown over, high winds will also increase fuel bills. A row of trees at a respectable non-shadow-casting distance is a great help.

**3 Frost** Cold air, like water, always seeks the lowest level, so don't build a greenhouse in a dip or at the foot of a slope. In such a frost pocket heating bills will be higher and the plants will grow more slowly.

**4 Drainage** Choose a piece of well-drained land – especially if you want to be able to get to your greenhouse on wet days and also if you want to grow plants in the border soil.

**5 Level** The foundations will be much easier and cheaper to lay and the greenhouse more easily erected if the site is level.

**6 Services** If you want water and electricity laid on in your greenhouse, don't site it at the far end of the garden. The nearer it is to the house, the cheaper it will be to connect up the vital supplies. Access in wet weather will also be less uncomfortable the nearer the greenhouse is to the back door.

**7 Orientation** Many experts recommend siting the traditional greenhouse so that the ridge runs east/west. If this fits in with your plans, fair enough. If it doesn't, don't worry. Many excellent plants are grown in greenhouses running in all directions. Lean-to houses can be attached to walls with any aspect. A south-facing lean-to will get the most sun, but one facing north will still grow a surprisingly wide range of plants.

## Foundations

All greenhouses, apart from polythene structures, should be built on some kind of foundation to ensure stability. Today, many manufacturers supply precast concrete sections which, when fitted together, form the right size base for their range of greenhouses. Provided that the ground is firm and level, and the greenhouse is securely bolted to these sections, good anchorage is achieved and the onerous task of laying concrete foundations is avoided.

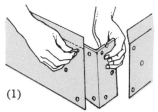

(1)

(3)

**How to assemble a steel base**

(1) Bolt the base together. (2) Put the base in a shallow trench and check the level. (3) Make sure the base is square. (4) Put some concrete at each corner to hold the base permanently in position

The precast concrete sectional base comes in separate pieces that easily fit together

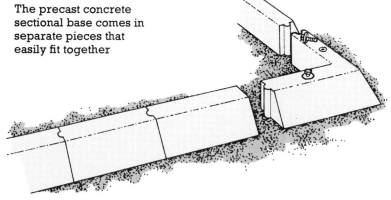

12

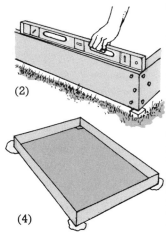

(2)

(4)

Some firms offer steel bases for their greenhouses. These are quite strong, but not heavy enough to hold the greenhouse down in high winds. This means that they must be anchored to the soil either with concrete, or with stout metal stakes.

If the greenhouse is not supplied with foundations, you will have to construct some yourself, or arrange for a local builder to do so. You can either lay a single course of bricks on a bed of cement over rammed hard core, or a mixture of 6 parts aggregate to 1 part sand and 1 part cement, mixed together with water to a moist but firm consistency, will set to form a solid concrete foundation. Sink two or three coach bolts into the concrete on each side, with their threaded ends uppermost. Corresponding holes drilled in the base plates will enable you to fasten the greenhouse to the foundations when it has been erected.

### Timber treatment

Aluminium greenhouses need nothing in the way of treatment before erection. Timber houses may need to be painted with preservative if they were not dipped in it during manufacture, and this should be done quite thoroughly before they are erected.

### Putting the greenhouse together

Manufacturers provide quite detailed instructions on how to erect their greenhouses, and may even offer a free erection service – which is well worth taking advantage of. If you have to do the job yourself, get a friend to help you.

After spreading damp-proof coursing material such as roofing felt along the foundations, one end section is placed in position first and a side section is bolted to it. The other side and end sections are then attached and, finally, the roof panels are bolted into position.

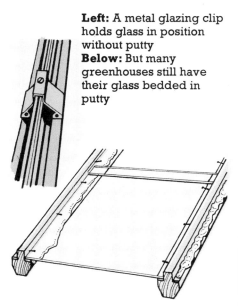

**Left:** A metal glazing clip holds glass in position without putty
**Below:** But many greenhouses still have their glass bedded in putty

### Glazing

On most greenhouses, 24oz (or 3mm) horticultural grade glass is used. Many greenhouses are provided with plastic glazing strips or metal clips, which means that the glass can be attached to the framework without putty. If putty has to be used, work it well into the rebates along the glazing bars, press the glass into position, tap in glazing brads to hold it firm and then trim off the excess putty. Wipe putty marks off the glass immediately.

Always glaze one strip of the greenhouse from bottom to top at a time, working down the length of the house, and try to complete the job on a calm day. This is not always possible, but a greenhouse left half glazed can be severely buffeted and damaged by wind.

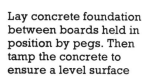

Lay concrete foundation between boards held in position by pegs. Then tamp the concrete to ensure a level surface

# Greenhouses

Whether or not you decide to heat your greenhouse will depend entirely on the plants you want to grow. An unheated structure offers enough protection to some seedlings and tender plants during late spring and summer, and to hardy bulbs and plants in winter, but it will not have the ability to keep out severe frosts. For this reason, some form of heating is necessary to keep the temperature above freezing point in any greenhouse where tender plants are to be overwintered. Where plants preferring a consistently warm environment are grown, this heating must be continued through most of the year.

There are many ways of heating a greenhouse, but the following systems are the most effective:

## Boilers

An oil, gas or solid fuel boiler connected to a system of water-filled heating pipes is the bulkiest and most expensive system to install, but it is also one of the most effective for larger greenhouses, say, over 3m (10ft) wide and 4·5m (15ft) long. The boiler is usually sited outside the greenhouse at the door end – under cover to protect it from wind and rain – and the 5cm (2in) or 10cm (4in) diameter water-filled pipes run through the wall and around the edge of the greenhouse near to the floor.

A solid fuel boiler standing outside the greenhouse heats water which then runs through pipes inside

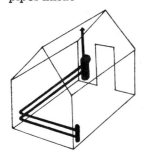

The type of boiler you choose will depend on which fuel is most convenient to use. Oil and solid fuel have to be stored, but gas can be piped straight from the main. The size of boiler and length of pipes needed will be governed by the size of the greenhouse and the temperature at which it is to be kept.

## Electric heaters

By far the cleanest and most easily controlled heaters are those which use electricity. Unfortunately, they are the most expensive to run. Tubular radiators and fan heaters are the most popular types and both should be fitted with thermostats for maximum efficiency and economy. (See p.19.) The dry heat produced by these appliances is beneficial in winter when moisture-loving fungus diseases can be a problem.

**Below: A thermostatically controlled electric fan heater is expensive to run but easy to control**

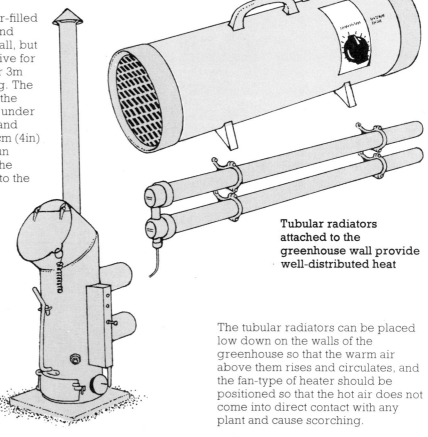

Tubular radiators attached to the greenhouse wall provide well-distributed heat

The tubular radiators can be placed low down on the walls of the greenhouse so that the warm air above them rises and circulates, and the fan-type of heater should be positioned so that the hot air does not come into direct contact with any plant and cause scorching.

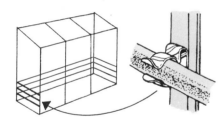

**Heating cables held in place by clips are suitable for heating small areas where a larger heater would be too powerful**

Electric soil- or air-warming cables have an advantage over tubular and fan heaters in that they are much cheaper to run. The special plastic-covered wire is plugged into the electricity supply and the current causes it to heat up. Fastened to the framework in a mini-lean-to greenhouse or a small free-standing one, warming cables will produce sufficient heat to keep out frost, whereas any larger heater would be much too powerful and cause overheating.

All electrical equipment in the greenhouse is potentially dangerous and must be connected up either by a professional electrician or by someone who is experienced in such matters. Never use domestic electrical equipment in the greenhouse – it will not be safe in the humid and wet environment.

## Paraffin heaters

The fact that they are relatively cheap to buy and to run has made paraffin heaters very popular for use in the greenhouse.

They give off carbon dioxide, which plants can make use of, they can be used to boost other heating systems, and extension pipes can be fitted to assist in the distribution of heat. However, they do create a high humidity level, most cannot be

thermostatically controlled, and they can produce damaging fumes if not properly attended to.

Provided that a few rules are borne in mind, though, they can be used effectively with a wide range of plants. Remember to:

1 Buy a heater with a large enough output for your greenhouse.
2 Keep the heater on a firm and level base.
3 Keep the wick and other moving parts scrupulously clean and properly adjusted.
4 Keep the heater out of draughts.
5 Use only the best quality paraffin.
6 Use only a heater which is specifically designed for greenhouses (it will last longer and smell less).
7 Allow a little ventilation at all times when the heater is lit.

**Two types of paraffin heaters. These are economical to run and give out carbon dioxide which is valuable for plant growth**

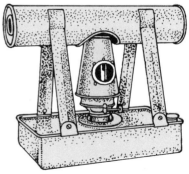

# Greenhouses

## Natural gas heaters

Certain types of heater are available which produce heat by burning natural gas. Like paraffin, they give off both carbon dioxide and water, and so create a humid atmosphere. Ventilation is necessary too to allow combustion to take place. Although natural gas will have to be laid on in the greenhouse, and the heater connected by a professional fitter, the advantages of thermostatic control and cheapness to run may place this heater high in the estimation of many gardeners.

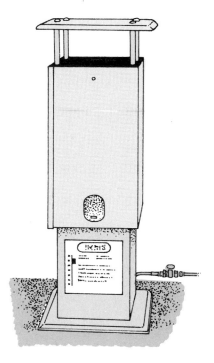

**Above:** A fluorescent strip light will enable you to work in the greenhouse during the winter evenings
**Right:** Several pieces of electrical equipment can be run in the greenhouse if a control box is fitted

**Left:** A thermostatically controlled natural gas heater can be an efficient answer to greenhouse heating if gas is already available

## What size heater?

When you have decided what kind of heater you would like to use, there are many long sums you can do to work out how big it needs to be. Such complicated calculations are not really necessary. In most cases the manufacturers of heating equipment will be only too pleased to advise you honestly on the size and type of heater you need for your greenhouse and your plants.

## Electricity

If your greenhouse is to be heated by electric tubular radiators or a fan heater, then a supply of electricity is obviously essential. But even if heating is achieved by other means, you will still find that electricity can do much to make life easier.

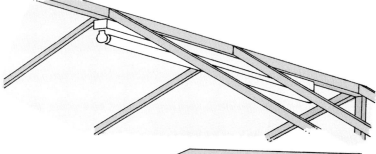

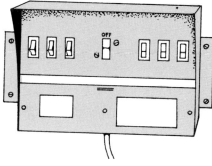

A single light bulb or a fluorescent tube suspended from the ridge of the house will provide good light when routine operations have to be carried out on winter evenings. Equipment such as soil-warming cables, mist propagation units, extractor fans, thermostats and propagating cases all make plant raising easier and strengthen the case for laying on electricity in the greenhouse.

Connecting up the supply and fitting the power points to the inside of the greenhouse is the one job you should not do yourself – seek the help of a competent electrician. Heavy-duty cables have to be laid statutory distances above or below soil level and well-insulated power points fitted firmly to the greenhouse framework. Water is always around and the fittings used have to be able to withstand such conditions. If it is likely that two or more pieces of electrical equipment will be in use at any one time, you may consider having a control box fitted. This supplies as many power points as you want, together with a mains on/off switch in a protective casing.

## Conserving heat

As soon as you start to heat your greenhouse you will realise that there must be a cheaper way of enjoying yourself. But, if you've set your mind on growing plants which need some warmth, there is nothing you can do but look for ways of keeping your heating bills down.

Firstly, make sure that all doors and ventilators fit snugly. A howling draught can keep a thermostatically-controlled heater switched on for far longer than is necessary, and any plants situated in its cold wake may curl up and die. Make sure the glass is clean so that every last drop of sunlight reaches the plants, and position heating equipment so that its benefit is felt the entire length of the house.

If your greenhouse is heated through the winter to a temperature of 10°C (50°F) or more, it will be worth investing in some form of insulation to prevent heat loss. The type of greenhouse you have will determine the amount of heat lost. Timbered sides offer better insulation than those made of glass.

Some manufacturers have provided a solution to this problem in the form of insulating panels which can be fitted to the sides of glass-to-ground greenhouses. They are easily attached to the frame of the house.

If no form of ready-made panels is available, then you will have to rig something up yourself. Double glazing with glass is really out of the question due to cost and weight. The best course of action to take is to fit

**Ready-made plastic panels fixed to the lower frame provide some insulation during the winter months**

some thin polythene sheeting, which is as clear as possible, to the inside framework of the greenhouse so that a 2·5- or 5-cm (1- or 2-in) layer of air is completely trapped between polythene and glass. There is also a type of polythene which is covered in bubbles where air has been trapped between its two layers. It is more effective in preventing heat loss than ordinary polythene, though it does cost rather more.

The polythene will be easy to fix to a timber greenhouse with drawing pins, but in an aluminium house it will have to be attached either with adhesive tape when the framework is dry, or fitted to wooden frames which can be held in position with nuts and bolts.

However you manage to fix the insulating material, remember not to cover the ventilators; they will still be needed during bright sunshine. It is really not worth keeping your double glazing material in position after about April. By then, light will be as important to seedlings and plants as heat.

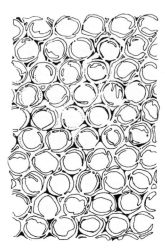

**'Bubble' polythene fixed to each bay of the green house provides valuable insulation but cuts down the natural light rather more than clear polythene sheeting**

# Greenhouses

During winter, all greenhouse owners are faced with the problem of keeping temperatures high enough to ensure that their plants survive. When summer comes, the situation is reversed and something has to be done to prevent the plants from being scorched by bright sunlight.

## Ventilation

Ventilation is the simplest and most effective answer to this problem. All greenhouses should be equipped with enough ventilators to give an adequate circulation of air throughout – the usual recommendation is that one ridge and one side ventilator should be fitted for every 2m (6ft) of the greenhouse's length. If you have a choice, pick the greenhouse with vents on both of its sides so that you can always allow air in on the side away from the wind.

Louvre vents are often fitted to the lower walls of the greenhouse to provide supplementary ventilation

Louvre units can often be purchased separately and fitted to many aluminium greenhouses in place of an ordinary pane of glass. When you're desperate to get air circulating, don't forget to open the door.

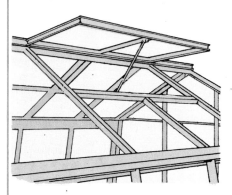

**A ventilator fitted with an ordinary adjustable casement stay**

There are various types of ventilator, the commonest consisting of a hinged frame equipped with a stay which adjusts the aperture. Sliding and louvre types are also offered, but check that these fit snugly when closed, for if badly made they can admit chilling draughts.

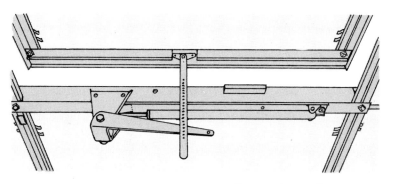

## Automated ventilation

The greenhouse temperature can often soar when you are not there to do anything about it, and for this reason you may be tempted to fit some kind of automatic device which will help out until you return.

The simplest and most useful piece of equipment in this respect is the automatic ventilating arm. Fitted to an ordinary ventilator, it can be preset to open it at a given temperature and to close it again when the air cools. The unit is not powered in any way, but it is activated by the expansion of a cylinder of petroleum jelly which operates a system of levers, so opening the vent.

Automatic ventilators are the answer if you are out at work all day, as they open and close according to the temperature in the greenhouse

## Fan cooling

Fans are another help in circulating greenhouse air. A simple one mounted high up at the far end of the house will ensure good air movement, and an extractor-type fitted with louvres can lower the greenhouse temperature even more rapidly. As with louvred ventilators, beware of draughts from this fixture in winter.

## Thermostats

Many electric heaters in particular are supplied with built-in thermostats which make for much greater economy. Fan and tubular heaters can be preset to switch on and off at a variety of temperatures to keep conditions in the greenhouse as stable as possible.

If your electric heater is not fitted with a thermostat, consider buying one separately and having it wired into your system.

The rod-type thermostat is the most popular and it should be attached to the inside of the greenhouse among the plants, but shaded from direct sunlight.

## Shading

Ventilators are fine for improving air circulation and reducing temperatures to a certain extent, but they can do nothing to protect the plants from scorching sunshine. For this reason, it is usual to provide some kind of shield between the sun and the plants in summer, usually on the south-facing sides of the greenhouse. The cheapest way of doing this is to coat the glass with a shading compound. The kinds which form a white coating are preferable to those which are green for they reflect the light more efficiently.

There are two shading preparations of this kind which have worthwhile advantages. One, called Coolglass, is electrostatic and clings so fiercely to the glass that it cannot be washed off by rain, yet when dry it can be

removed with a duster. Varied concentrations of it can be mixed to give light or heavy shading. The other preparation, Vari-shade, is white when dry, but translucent when wet, so allowing light to enter on rainy summer days when shading is not necessary.

More permanent, but consequently more expensive, shading can be achieved with blinds made of plastic-strips, plastic netting or bamboo. Ideally these should be positioned on the outside of the greenhouse so that they intercept the sunlight before it has a chance to lift the temperature. Against this must be set the fact that they are easier to fix inside the greenhouse, ventilators are more easily operated than when blinds are fitted externally, and damage by wind and rain is not encountered.

If you can fix the blinds outside, attach them so that ventilators can still be opened, and remove them to the safety of a shed or garage through the winter.

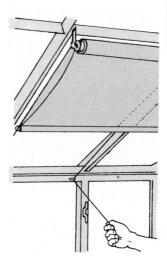

Internal blinds are one answer to shading in the greenhouse

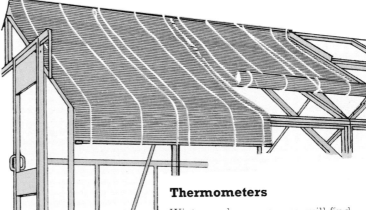

**External slatted blinds keep the temperature lower more effectively than internal blinds but can be damaged by wind**

## Thermometers

Winter and summer you will find great comfort in a thermometer! The maximum and minimum type is fitted with needles which tell you what the temperature rose to during the day and what it fell to at night, and on this information you can adjust your heating and/or ventilating system. Position the thermometer in a spot where air circulates well, but out of direct sunlight.

# Greenhouses

Exactly where in the greenhouse the plants should be placed depends on their habit and the kind of environment they prefer.

## Soil borders

Many experts are inclined to throw up their hands in horror at the thought of growing plants in the borders of the greenhouse. The reason for this is that such practice is supposed to lead to trouble in the form of disease attack or soil sickness. The alternative usually given is that the soil should be removed to a spade's depth, the trench lined with polythene, perforated to allow drainage, and then filled with sterilized compost such as John Innes.

Such action, apart from costing a small fortune, is really unnecessary unless the soil is known to be contaminated. The greenhouse gardener is probably far better off using the natural border soil for a few years (and varying the crops he grows in it) and replacing it if and when it shows signs of being infected. Provided that fertilizer and well-rotted manure are incorporated, the plants are likely to thrive. Tomatoes, peppers, aubergines, chrysanthemums, grape vines, peaches and many climbing plants can be grown well in the greenhouse border.

## Pathways

A precast concrete slab path down the centre of the greenhouse will prevent undue trampling of the border soil and will provide a sound base on which to stand when attending to plants. Gravel is an alternative and this can be drenched with a hose in summer to moisten the atmosphere.

## Staging

Some kind of flat or, in wide houses, tiered benching will provide a good home for most greenhouse plants. The prime requirement of staging is

that it should be sturdy. Pots full of compost are surprisingly heavy when grouped together.

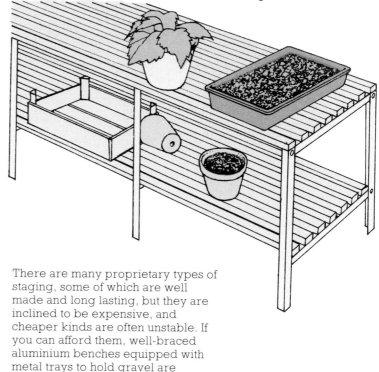

Staging consisting of wooden slats must be strong enough to support the weight of pots and compost

There are many proprietary types of staging, some of which are well made and long lasting, but they are inclined to be expensive, and cheaper kinds are often unstable. If you can afford them, well-braced aluminium benches equipped with metal trays to hold gravel are probably the best kind to buy. The width you choose will depend on the space between the side wall of your

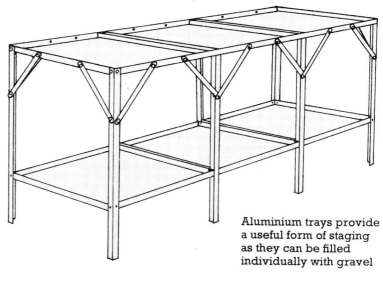

Aluminium trays provide a useful form of staging as they can be filled individually with gravel

greenhouse and the door, but 1m (3ft) is about the maximum distance over which it is comfortable to lean. If you are a bit of a do-it-yourselfer, you can save a lot of money by making your own timber staging.

Shade-loving plants such as ferns can be set on a layer of gravel on the border soil. Whether or not you spread gravel on the staging is up to you. It gives additional humidity in summer when the air is dry, but it can hold on to unwanted moisture in winter. If you wish, place gravel in moveable plastic trays which can be used during the summer and removed in winter.

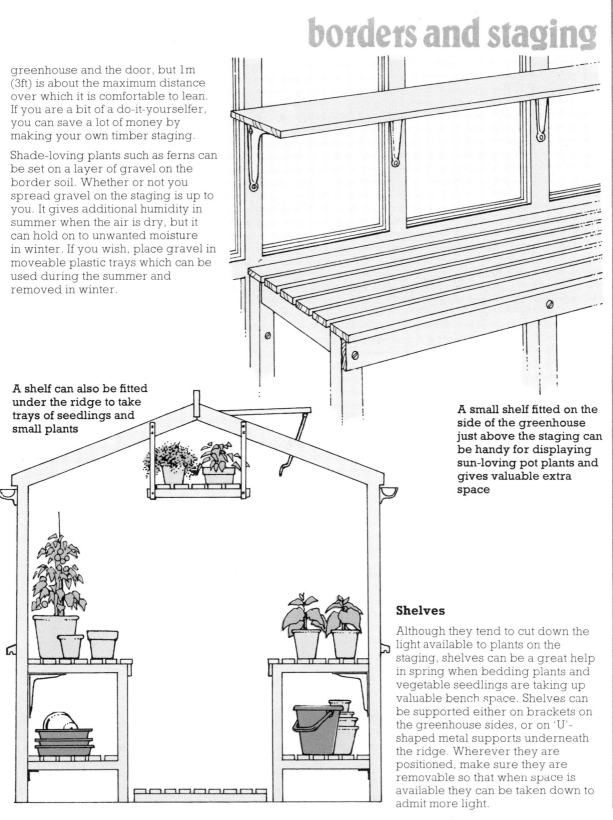

**A shelf can also be fitted under the ridge to take trays of seedlings and small plants**

**A small shelf fitted on the side of the greenhouse just above the staging can be handy for displaying sun-loving pot plants and gives valuable extra space**

### Shelves

Although they tend to cut down the light available to plants on the staging, shelves can be a great help in spring when bedding plants and vegetable seedlings are taking up valuable bench space. Shelves can be supported either on brackets on the greenhouse sides, or on 'U'-shaped metal supports underneath the ridge. Wherever they are positioned, make sure they are removable so that when space is available they can be taken down to admit more light.

# Greenhouses

The task of watering may seem to be a simple one, but it is true to say that more plants are killed by being kept too wet than by any other means. If healthy plants are to be raised, the skills of watering must be mastered.

## When to water

Nine times out of ten, the answer to the question 'How often do I water my so-and-so?' is 'When it is dry'. There are a few plants, such as azaleas, which must never be allowed to dry out completely. Cacti, on the other hand, can be left dry for longer periods than most plants.

There are several tests you can make to find out whether a plant is dry or not:

**1** Weigh the pot in your hand. If it is dry it will feel quite light.

**2** Clay pots can be tapped with a wooden cotton reel attached to a cane. If the pot is dry it will give out a ringing sound; if it is moist, only a dull thud. Beware of using this method on cracked pots for it will not work.

**3** Look at and feel the surface of the soil in the pot. Sometimes it may dry out when the body of the soil is quite damp, but usually it is a good guide.

**4** In greenhouse borders, remove some soil with a trowel to see if it is dry a few inches down.

**5** If you are a real coward you can resort to using one of the many soil-moisture meters offered for sale. These tell you, with the aids of lights, bleeps or a pointer, whether the soil is wet or dry.

It is never a good idea to water plants at regular intervals. On bright sunny days, the compost in the pot is bound to dry out more quickly than in cloudy weather. When you do decide to water, give sufficient to soak the container right through. When plants are grown in pots, a gap should be left between the rim of the pot and the surface of the compost to allow water to be poured in.

Remember that plants will usually recover if they wilt due to under-watering, but if they wilt due to overwatering they will seldom pull round.

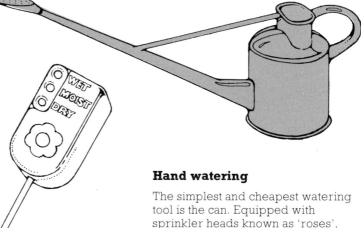

**The simple watering can, one of the most valuable tools in the greenhouse**

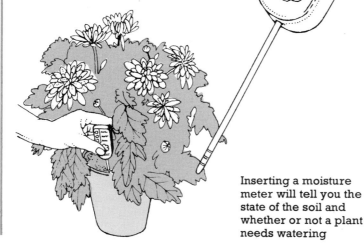

**Inserting a moisture meter will tell you the state of the soil and whether or not a plant needs watering**

## Hand watering

The simplest and cheapest watering tool is the can. Equipped with sprinkler heads known as 'roses', watering cans may be used to water seedlings without knocking them down or displacing the compost, and also to 'damp down'. This is carried out in most greenhouses during spring and summer when additional humidity is beneficial. Water is simply sprayed on paths and benches and as it evaporates it moistens the atmosphere.

Water may be used either straight from the tap (preferably fitted in the greenhouse), or from a storage tank positioned under the staging. If this is filled by rainwater from the greenhouse guttering, fit some kind of filter over the inlet to keep out leaves and other debris which may foul the water.

## Automatic watering

If you have to be out all day and find that the time you spend in your greenhouse is limited, an automatic watering system may be just what you need. There are many different types, but the capillary bench is perhaps the best. This used to consist of a bed of sand but now units are available which use plastic fibre matting. This is laid across a tray so one end of it rests in a reservoir of

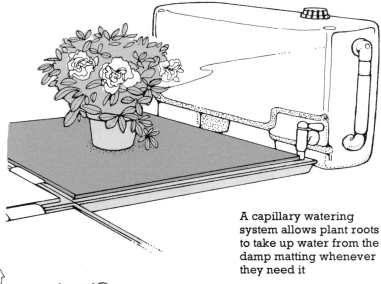

A capillary watering system allows plant roots to take up water from the damp matting whenever they need it

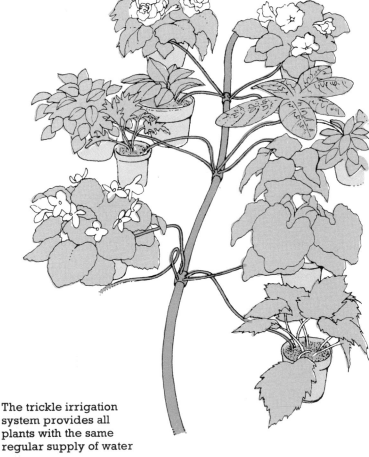

The trickle irrigation system provides all plants with the same regular supply of water

water, kept topped up by a plastic tank. The matting draws water throughout its length and the plants standing on it, provided that the compost in the pots is in contact with the matting, can draw up what moisture they need. The matting does have a tendency to become coated with green algae, but there are chemicals which can be used to prevent this.

Plastic pots can be used quite effectively with capillary watering, but clay pots must be provided with a wick, instead of crocks, which can take the water to the compost. A short strip of the matting material leading through the hole will do the trick.

Other systems of automatic watering use small-bore pipes which can be led to each plant in the greenhouse and through which water is propelled at regular intervals. Although this system saves time, it is unlikely that all the plants will have the same water requirement, and some are bound to be over- or under-watered.

# Greenhouses

The gardeners of old were perfectionists who insisted that every type of plant needed its own special compost, but modern research has shown otherwise, and we are now fortunate in having just a few potting and seed-sowing composts which will grow most plants to perfection. The main requirements of a compost are good drainage, adequate moisture retention, and a supply of plant nutrients.

## John Innes composts

Named after the research institute where they were first formulated, the John Innes seed and potting composts are now manufactured by many firms. To be sure of buying compost which is made up to the original specification, look for the mark of the John Innes Manufacturers' Association on the bag.

**J.I. seed compost:** Use this as a medium in which to sow all seeds. Seedlings will remain green and healthy for several weeks after germination.

**J.I. No. 1 potting compost:** Pot up newly rooted cuttings and grow bedding plants in this medium.

**J.I. No. 2 potting compost:** Ideal for most pot plants, this contains twice as much fertilizer as No. 1.

**J.I. No. 3 potting compost:** Offers three times as much fertilizer as No. 1. Suitable for large and vigorous pot plants, tomatoes, cucumbers and melons. Do not be tempted to pot young plants in this or No. 2, it will not make them grow any faster.

**J.I. Ericaceous compost:** Made up of the same ingredients as the other potting composts but lime is omitted, making it suitable for lime-hating plants such as rhododendrons and heathers.

Never store these composts for longer than you have to; two months is the recommended maximum (especially as you don't know how long they have been in the bag). After this time they begin to turn sour.

## Soilless composts

Most of these are based on peat and contain fertilizer and sometimes a little sand. They are light and clean to use, but their nutrients are exhausted by the plant more quickly than those in John Innes compost and so plants will need regular feeding about six weeks after being potted up. Tall plants will often overbalance if potted in soilless compost as it is so lightweight.

When potting with soilless mixtures, firm the compost only lightly and never allow it to dry out completely, for it is difficult to wet again. Soilless mixtures seldom become compacted so crocking is unnecessary. Always store the compost in a cool, dark place so that it remains moist.

## Cutting compost

This is an easy compost to make at home. Mix together granulated peat and sharp sand in equal parts. Cuttings need no more than a moist but well-drained medium in which to root and this mixture fits the bill.

Always avoid using bright yellow builders' sand in any compost, for it contains fungi and other undesirable impurities.

## Ring culture

If your greenhouse is erected on a piece of land with poor soil, if the soil is exhausted, or if the house has a solid concrete floor, you will not be able to plant things in the ground. This makes the job of growing the gardener's favourite greenhouse crop, tomatoes, that much more difficult. They can be cultivated in pots, but the amount of nutrition they can find is rather limited and the yield will be reduced. You may resort to planting them in growing

Cross-section through a ring-culture system showing the two types of roots developed by the tomato plant. The fibrous feeding roots form in the soil while the thick white roots take up water from the aggregate

bags (plastic bags of peaty compost), and this is a good idea, but it can be expensive.

Ring culture offers the ideal solution. Most of the equipment needed can be used again and the plants should fruit exceptionally well. The first requirement is a bed of washed pea shingle 15cm (6in) deep. This can be laid either in a 15-cm (6-in) trench in the greenhouse border, or on top of the soil or floor, retained by boards. Ashes can be used in place of the gravel, but they should be exposed to the elements for a few months before use to clear out any impurities. Peat is sometimes recommended, but tomatoes can become stunted and yellowed by it; gravel is a cheap and clean solution.

The rings are usually made of aluminium or bitumen impregnated cardboard, but you can make your own by cutting the bottoms out of plastic pots with a hacksaw blade.

Ideally the rings should be about 23cm (9in) in diameter and 23cm (9in) deep. Set the rings on the gravel 45cm (18in) apart and fill them to within a couple of inches of their rims with John Innes No. 3 or a soilless potting compost a few days before you intend to put in the young plants, so the compost warms up.

When the plants are ready for planting out water them well, tap them from their pots, and plant them quite firmly, one to each ring. Water them in well so that the soil is settled and uniformly moist. From now on any water you apply should be poured on the gravel, and it is as well to give it a drench every day.

Stake the plants and feed them every week or ten days with a diluted liquid fertilizer as soon as the flowers have fallen from the first truss. Remember: Food goes into the pot and water goes on to the gravel.

At the end of the season, soak the gravel to remove any impurities and wash aluminium or plastic rings; both can be used again.

# Greenhouses

Most seeds and cuttings will grow and root far more readily in a warm, humid environment than in one which is cold and damp, but to heat the greenhouse to a suitable temperature would be very costly and the conditions would be undesirable for other plants. This is where the propagating case, or frame, comes into its own.

The unit consists of a heated bed of sand, on which pots and seed trays can be stood, or a rooting medium in which cuttings can be inserted. Raised sides retain the mixture, and glass or plastic is placed over the top to keep in heat and maintain a moist atmosphere which will prevent cuttings from wilting and seedlings from drying out.

Various types of propagating cases are available. The simplest consists of a seed tray, topped with a transparent plastic cover about 15cm (6in) high, which is fitted with small

**An electrically controlled propagator with glass sliding doors can be used as a terrarium as well as for raising seedlings and cuttings**

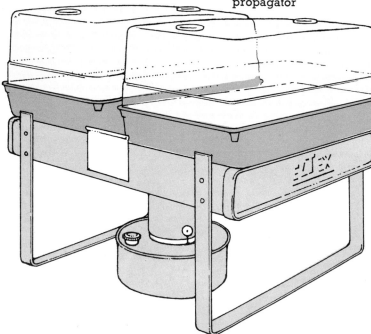

**There is room for two propagating trays to sit on this paraffin-heated propagator**

vents. To raise the temperature in the unit, an electrically heated base can be positioned under the tray. The same covered trays can also be placed on top of a specially adapted paraffin heater, and this unit may suit you if your greenhouse is not supplied with electricity. The best kind of propagator is one which incorporates a thermostat, and such units can either be bought complete, or made much more cheaply at home.

If you want to make a propagator yourself, a rectangular wooden frame 20cm (8in) deep can be fitted with electric soil-warming cables which will provide the necessary heat. Lay the plastic-covered cable on a 5-cm (2-in) deep layer of sand, spreading it out in even loops, and fasten two or three circuits around the side of the frame near the top to heat the air a little. Manufacturers of cables will give an indication as to what length will be needed to heat a given area. For most home propagating, a temperature of 16° to 18°C (60° to 65°F) will be sufficient.

On top of the cable you can either place sand, on which trays and pots containing seeds and cuttings can be stood, or you can fill the frame to within about 10cm (4in) of its rim with a rooting medium, such as vermiculite or a mixture of peat and sand in equal parts, and cuttings can be inserted directly into this. A rod-type thermostat can be easily wired up to the cable, and it can be set to maintain a given temperature. Both you and the seeds or cuttings will benefit from this – it provides a better environment for them and it saves money for you. If the cuttings or seeds are in trays and pots stood on sand, the thermostat should be positioned to control the air temperature. If cuttings are dibbed into a rooting medium in the frame, then the thermostat should run through it to control the temperature at the plants' roots.

The frame can be topped either with a sheet of glass or a shroud of polythene supported on a wire framework. Whichever material is used, remove it occasionally and clear it of condensation.

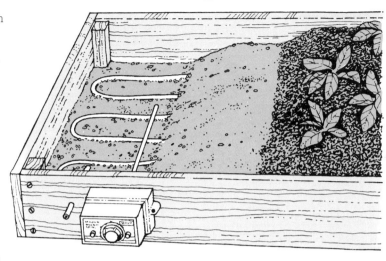

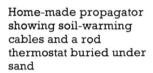

**Mist propagator showing soil-warming cables which heat the rooting medium and an electronic leaf to control the mist spray**

**Home-made propagator showing soil-warming cables and a rod thermostat buried under sand**

A little ventilation is beneficial at all times to keep the air fresh, and as the cuttings or seedlings get going, more air can be allowed in and the temperature gradually reduced to harden them off. Keep the sand or the rooting medium moist at all times so that the heat is effectively conducted and the plants do not dehydrate.

### Mist propagation

Many cuttings which are difficult to root can be persuaded to cooperate if they are sprayed with water from time to time, and a mist propagation unit is an automated system of doing just that. By keeping the leaves and stems of cuttings moist, it reduces their water loss and speeds up rooting.

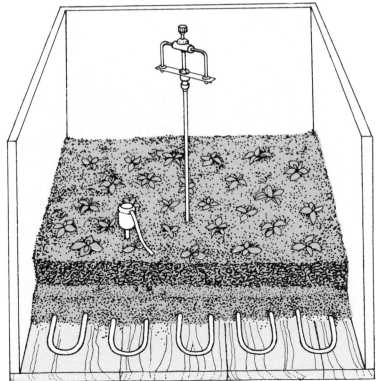

An atomising jet is positioned over the plants and when a piece of moisture-sensitive plastic containing two electrodes dries out, the water is switched on until this 'electronic leaf' is wet again. Positioned in a topless propagating frame fitted with soil-warming cables, this system is of great value.

# Greenhouses

## Seeds

Without a doubt, sowing seeds is one of the cheapest ways of raising plants. Packets of a wide range of flowers, fruits and vegetables can be bought for only a few pence and, in most cases, they will produce a large number of plants.

Most seeds are sown between January and March (the warmer your greenhouse the sooner you can start), and until sowing time they should be stored in a cool, dry, dark place. Always buy from a reputable source to make sure that you get good seed, and order early if you are choosing varieties from a catalogue so that you are not disappointed. Seeds freshly bought each year will give you the highest germination rate, but there are often some vegetable seeds left over at the end of the season and these might be worth saving. The list on the next page shows how long you can expect them to last.

## $F_1$ hybrids

Packets of seed which carry the description '$F_1$ hybrid' will be more expensive than the run-of-the-mill kinds which do not. This is because the seed was carefully produced by crossing two selected plants. The plants arising from the $F_1$ seed will be vigorous, uniform and will have the desirable qualities for which they were bred. If you, in turn, sow the seed saved from these $F_1$ hybrids it will not produce the same kind of plants. They will be varied and many of them will be inferior, and so $F_1$ varieties must be raised from freshly bought seed each year.

## Pelleted seeds

Many varieties of flower and vegetable seed are offered pelleted. The pellet consists of a type of clay, sometimes containing a fungicide to protect the seed, and it makes it easy to space the seeds out when sowing, so preventing overcrowding.

No seeds must ever be allowed to dry out during germination, but pelleted ones will often fail to come through at all if the soil moisture content is reduced only briefly.

## Sowing

To germinate, all seeds need a suitable temperature (16°–18°C (60°–65°F) will please most of them), a supply of moisture and a well-drained, airy compost. Always read the instructions on the packet before doing anything. Much valuable information is often crammed into just a few square inches of paper.

**Fill a seed tray with compost and firm the surface with a home-made presser. Then water the compost**

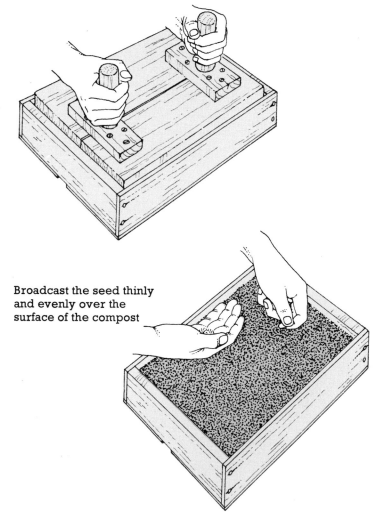

**Broadcast the seed thinly and evenly over the surface of the compost**

### Life of vegetable seeds

If you store your vegetable seeds in a cool, dry and dark place you can expect to use them for more than just one season's sowings. This is how long some of the popular kinds will last:

| Seed | Years | Seed | Years | Seed | Years |
|------|-------|------|-------|------|-------|
| Aubergine | 5 | Cucumber | 5-6 | Pepper | 4 |
| Beans | 3 | Endive | 5 | Pumpkin | 4 |
| Beetroot | 4 | Kale | 5 | Radish | 5 |
| Broccoli | 5 | Kohl rabi | 5 | Salsify | 2 |
| Brussels sprouts | 5 | Leek | 3 | Scorzonera | 2 |
| Cabbage | 4-5 | Lettuce | 4-5 | Seakale | 1-2 |
| Carrot | 3-4 | Marrow | 5-6 | Spinach | 5 |
| Cauliflower | 4-5 | Melon | 5 | Squash | 5 |
| Celeriac | 5 | Onion | 1-2 | Sweet corn | 1-2 |
| Celery | 5-6 | Parsley | 2-3 | Swiss chard | 4 |
| Chicory | 5 | Parsnip | 1-2 | Tomato | 4 |
| Chinese cabbage | 5 | Pea | 3 | Turnip | 5 |

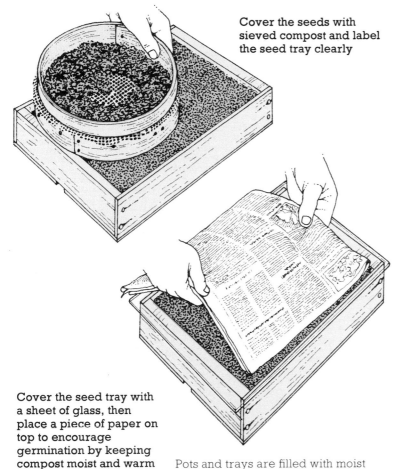

**Cover the seeds with sieved compost and label the seed tray clearly**

**Cover the seed tray with a sheet of glass, then place a piece of paper on top to encourage germination by keeping compost moist and warm**

Pots and trays are filled with moist compost and lightly but evenly firmed, first with the fingers and then with the base of another plant pot or with a home-made presser, so that

the surface of the compost is 1cm ($\frac{1}{2}$in) below the rim of the container to allow for watering. John Innes and soilless seed composts are both suitable.

Moisten the compost further at this stage to avoid watering after sowing. Either soak each container using a watering can fitted with a fine rose, or stand them all in a shallow tray of water until fresh moisture can be seen on the surface. All seeds should be sown thinly and evenly and most need a covering of compost. This is best rubbed through a 0·5-cm ($\frac{1}{4}$-in) sieve – you can stop sieving as soon as the seeds disappear from view.

Dust-fine seeds such as begonia, lobelia, petunia and calceolaria should not be covered at all. Large seeds such as runner beans can be sown individually 2·5cm (1in) deep in pots. They can be planted straight into the garden with undisturbed roots as soon as they are large enough and the weather is amenable.

After sowing, label each container to show the variety and the date sown (the latter so that you know when to give up hope – but remember that some seeds take several weeks to germinate) and cover first with a sheet of glass and then a sheet of newspaper. Most seeds germinate better in the even, humid atmosphere these two coverings provide. If you have a propagator, place the sown trays or pots in it. If not, put them on the staging near the greenhouse heater.

Check all the containers *every* day and turn the glass to remove condensation. If you forget to look for just one day, the seedlings could be through and they will become tall and spindly in a matter of hours. As soon as the first one is through, remove the glass and paper. Water with a can fitted with a fine rose if the soil starts to dry out and protect the seedlings from bright sunshine with single sheets of newspaper.

# Greenhouses

## Pricking out

As soon as the seedlings are large enough to be picked up with your finger and thumb without being crushed they can be pricked out. This involves transplanting them to a wider spacing in trays of potting compost. Some seedlings, such as begonias, are so small that they have to be dug up with a pointed stick and settled into their new container using the end of it.

Fill and firm the trays as before and mark out the spot to be occupied by each seedling using a dibber (if you don't possess one, a pencil is just as good). Allow about 4cm (1½in) between them and you will get about 35 seedlings (5 × 7) in a plastic tray. Prise the seedlings from their compost with the dibber or pencil and lift each by holding one of its leaves between your finger and thumb. Dib a hole in the new tray of compost, lower the roots in and firm back the soil with the dibber.

Certain plants can be pricked out direct into 8-cm (3-in) pots (tomatoes are an example) but most bedding plants and vegetables are quite happy in trays. Water the seedlings well into their new home and label them again. The seedlings will quickly develop into sturdy young plants as long as good ventilation, good light and a moderate temperature is provided.

## Division

Plants which send up lots of shoots from below ground, eventually turning into a thick clump, can be easily propagated by dividing them up into pieces which consist of at least one shoot and a portion of the root system. Many ferns are best increased by this method of propagation, and with all suitable plants it is best carried out in spring.

Knock the plant to be divided out of its pot, tease off any loose soil and either pull the plant to pieces carefully with your hands, or cut it

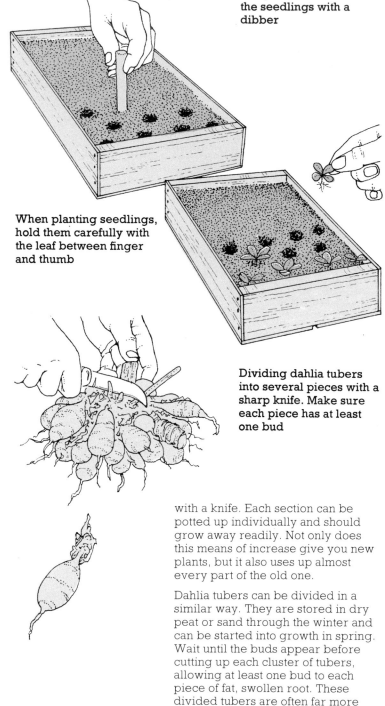

After firming the compost, make holes for the seedlings with a dibber

When planting seedlings, hold them carefully with the leaf between finger and thumb

Dividing dahlia tubers into several pieces with a sharp knife. Make sure each piece has at least one bud

with a knife. Each section can be potted up individually and should grow away readily. Not only does this means of increase give you new plants, but it also uses up almost every part of the old one.

Dahlia tubers can be divided in a similar way. They are stored in dry peat or sand through the winter and can be started into growth in spring. Wait until the buds appear before cutting up each cluster of tubers, allowing at least one bud to each piece of fat, swollen root. These divided tubers are often far more vigorous than those left alone.

## Plantlets

Greenhouse plants which have a do-it-yourself method of increase make life particularly easy for the gardener. The spider plant (chlorophytum), the pick-a-back plant (tolmiea) and the mother of thousands (saxifraga) all produce plantlets on long or short stems. Propagation is a simple matter of cutting the baby from the stem and encouraging its roots to grow in a mixture of peat and sand, or even in water. Do this at any time of year and pot up your new plants as soon as they have made a small cluster of roots.

## Cuttings

Many plants do not produce seeds, others do so infrequently, and modern hybrids will give rise to varied and inferior offspring. If such plants cannot be propagated by division or plantlets either, some other means must be used. Cuttings can provide the answer.

**Softwood cuttings** Taken in spring or summer when plants are in active growth and the stem tissue is still soft, this type of cutting can be used to increase dahlias, chrysanthemums, fuchsias and many greenhouse and house plants.

Select vigorous and healthy young shoots on the plants you want to increase, and remove them with about four leaf joints or 'nodes'. Prepare the cuttings by removing the lower leaves and making a clean cut below a node with a sharp knife or a razor blade. The finished cutting should be 5 to 8cm (2 to 3in) long and half its stem should be free of leaves.

Tradescantias, begonias, impatiens (busy lizzie) and other easily rooted cuttings can be stood in jam jars of water and potted up when they have formed roots an inch or so long.

Cuttings of other plants are best rooted in cutting compost (see p.24). First dip just the stem bases in hormone rooting powder and tap off the excess. Insert the prepared cuttings to half their length either in the compost in a propagator, or in pots. Four or five will be happy dibbed in around the edge of a 10-cm (4-in) pot, watered in and then either stood in the propagator to root or covered with a polythene bag and placed in a warm part of the greenhouse. What most of them like is a fairly humid atmosphere and a temperature around 16° to 18°C (60° to 65°F). Give them protection from bright sunlight too.

Cuttings vary in the time they take to root, but the shoots of most of them will start to grow when roots have formed. Pot them up as soon as possible after rooting.

Rooting a plantlet of chlorophytum in a glass of water. When roots have formed, sever 'baby' from parent plant and pot up

**Left:** Preparing a soft-wood cutting of pelargonium
**Below:** Insert several cuttings round the edge of each pot

# Greenhouses

**Half-ripe cuttings** When shoots on many plants begin to harden during July and August, they are said to be half-ripe or semi-ripe. Cuttings taken at this time of year can be prepared so that they are slightly longer than softwood types (about 10cm (4in)) and rooted in exactly the same way. Most garden shrubs are best propagated from half-ripe cuttings and these can be overwintered in the greenhouse and hardened off the following spring before being planted outside.

Half-ripe cuttings of some shrubs may root better if they are torn from a mature stem with what is known as a 'heel'. The heel is trimmed of its tail and dipped in rooting powder before being inserted into the compost.

**Taking a cutting with a heel. The cutting is torn off the parent plant and the heel trimmed before being inserted in the rooting medium**

Streptocarpus (Cape primrose) leaves are long and narrow and if these are cut into sections and inserted in cutting compost they will form roots and shoots at the point of the large central vein. Take care to ensure that the cut end which was nearest the crown of the plant is inserted.

*Begonia rex* can be propagated in two ways. The leaves can be laid out flat on a bed of moist sand in a propagator and the main veins cut through. If the medium is kept moist and the cut parts of the leaves remain in contact with it (weighing them down with two or three pebbles helps), one new plant will arise at each cut. Alternatively, the leaf may be cut into 2·5-cm (1-in) squares and each square inserted vertically in the rooting medium. Again, make sure that each section is the right way up (the direction of the sap flow should be from the compost to the tip of the cutting).

**Leaf cuttings** Some plants can be increased during spring and summer from just a leaf, among them saintpaulias, streptocarpus and *Begonia rex*. All three of them can be rooted in different ways.

With saintpaulias (African violets), a leaf and its stalk is removed from the parent plant and the stalk is inserted vertically for its entire length in cutting compost. Rooting powder is unnecessary. In the humid atmosphere of a propagator or plastic bag, roots will soon be formed and a shoot will appear at the base of the leaf.

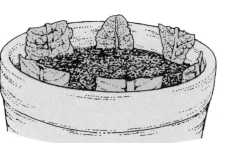

**Above:** Taking leaf cuttings of streptocarpus. Cut the leaf into sections **Left:** Make sure the area nearest the base of the leaf is inserted into the compost when potting up the cuttings

You do need patience for this method of propagation. Depending on the temperature (21°C (70°F) is ideal) roots will form either in a few weeks or a few months, but the polythene should not be removed until you can see a good cluster of white roots through it. The top part of the plant can be potted up, and you will probably find that the bottom half will form several lateral shoots which turn it, once more, into a desirable plant.

**Above:** Propagating *Begonia rex.*

**Below:** Air layering. (1) Make an upward incision (2) Fill with moist moss (3) Wrap area in polythene filled with more moist moss or peat

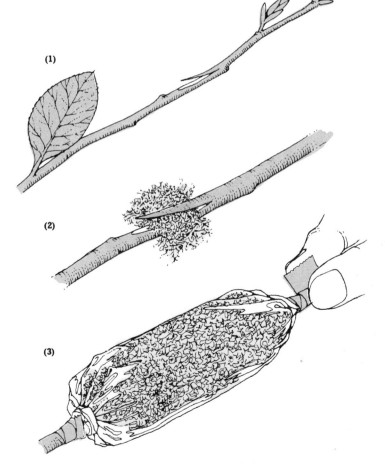

**Air layering** After several years, greenhouse and house plants can become so tall that they outgrow the space for which they were intended, or they may be only a few feet high when a sudden draught or water shortage causes them to shed their lower leaves creating an ugly bare stem. Air layering is the answer to this problem and it can be carried out in spring or summer on a good number of house plants, though the one most frequently demanding such treatment is the rubber plant, *Ficus elastica.*

An upward incision is made about 10cm (4in) from the lowest remaining leaf, or higher if you wish, to produce a cut 4cm (1½in) long at an angle of 45°. This is filled with moist sphagnum moss or coarse peat (though the latter is not so effective). Work some moss or peat around the stem at the same point and wrap the area in a 10-cm (4-in) wide strip of polythene, tying it top and bottom. Support the stem by fastening it above and below the cut to a stout cane pushed into the pot.

# Greenhouses

## Potting

The majority of greenhouse plants are grown in pots, and the job of planting them in these containers is known as potting. There are several confusing variations on this term and this is what they mean:

**Potting up:** Placing a rooted cutting or seedling in its first pot.

**Potting on:** Transferring a plant already in a pot to one of a larger size.

**Repotting:** Knocking the plant from its pot, removing some of the old soil, adding some new, and replanting it in the same container.

All kinds of potting are usually carried out in spring and summer when the plants are in active growth. Remember that plants should be well watered about an hour before the operation and the new pots should be clean.

Whether clay or plastic pots are used is up to you. Clay ones will need crocking (this involves placing a few broken pieces of pot, concave side downwards, over the basal hole). Both soilless and loam-based composts are suitable, but remember that large plants may overbalance in pots of light, soilless compost.

To pot a plant, choose a container large enough to hold the roots with just a little room to spare. Spread some compost in the bottom (over the crocks if they are required), sit the plant on this layer and work in more compost around the rootball. Push the compost down the inside of the pot with your fingers, firmly if it is loam-based, more gently if it is soilless. The level of the compost should finish between 1cm ($\frac{1}{2}$in) and 2·5cm (1in) below the rim depending on the size of the pot – the larger the pot the deeper the gap – and it should just cover the topmost roots of the plant. A good rap on a solid surface will settle the compost evenly.

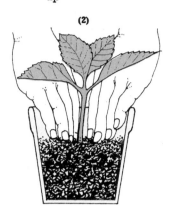

Potting up.
(1) Rest the plant on some compost in the base of the pot (2) Add more compost round the sides, firming it as you go (3) Plant correctly potted up

Never put a plant in a container too big for its roots; it will grow much more happily in one which it can quickly fill, for the compost will not have time to turn sour. After potting, water the plant well to settle it into its new home.

## Planting

Plant in growing bags and greenhouse borders just as you would in the garden. Take out a hole large enough to accommodate the roots and replace the soil, firming it (lightly in the growing bags) into position. Soak border soil before planting, growing bags after, and insert any stakes first to avoid damaging the roots.

## Feeding

Through spring and summer all plants in active growth can be fed about every ten days with a liquid fertilizer diluted in water. Always apply food when the soil in the pot of border is moist, for it can then go straight into action.

## Topdressing

This involves spreading a layer of rich compost over the surface of the soil in the pot or greenhouse border usually in spring or early summer. Plants which do not need potting on, or which resent root disturbance, can be given a good boost by removing a little of the compost from the surface of the pot and replacing it with something like John Innes No. 3 potting compost or its soilless equivalent.

Grapes, peaches, tomatoes, cucumbers and other plants grown in a greenhouse border will benefit from a more generous dressing of well-rotted manure or garden compost.

**White roots of cucumber showing above the surface of the compost. These must be covered as they appear**

**Chrysanthemums supported by a cane with a figure-of-eight tie**

## Plant supports

Not all plants have a sturdy habit, and many of them have been bred to produce large flower heads which their puny stems have no hope of holding up. So we have to step in and help them a bit. Canes provide a convenient means of holding up plants with single stems – split green ones for dainty plants and stouter whole ones for the heavies such as rubber plants and chrysanthemums. Push the cane in an inch or so from the stem of the plant and loop green garden twine or raffia (which ties much better if it is soaked first) once round the cane and then round the stem to form a figure-of-eight.

Bushy plants such as schizanthus can be supported with one or two small pieces of brushwood pushed into the soil, and many twining and climbing plants will take quickly either to an arch of wire, or to one of the many cane or plastic 'climbing frames' on the market. Choose types which will blend in rather than stand out as hideous eyesores.

Hyacinths can be held upright by having short lengths of stiff wire pushed through the stem and the bulb. Tomatoes can either be tied to stout canes, or wound around a length of strong twine (often known as fillis) which is tied between horizontal wires on the ground and the roof.

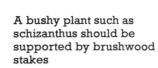

**A bushy plant such as schizanthus should be supported by brushwood stakes**

# Greenhouses

Cucumbers, peaches, vines and ornamental climbing plants are best tied in and trained to a framework of horizontal wires. This is supported a few inches from the glazing bars on the side and roof of the house by vine eyes. These eyed bolts or screws are easily fitted to a wooden house, but some means of attaching them to an aluminium framework will have to be devised. The wires should be spaced 23 to 30cm (9 to 12in) apart and they can be left in position permanently.

Supports for plants in growing bags are now readily available in the shops. Many of them are well constructed from sturdy, plastic-covered wire and with careful storage should last for many years.

## Stopping and training

Nearly all pot plants benefit from having the tips of their shoots pinched out or 'stopped' from time to time. Left to grow they soon become tall and spindly and their stems eventually flop over.

Dwarf plants and those which form almost stemless mounds of foliage obviously do not need this treatment, and where plants such as fuchsias and heliotrope are being grown as 'standards' – that is on a tall single stem – all sideshoots must be removed and the leading shoot left to

grow. This is finally pinched out when the main stem reaches the required height, and the shoots which arise are then treated just as you would a normal plant – pinching them out to encourage bushiness.

On cucumbers, melons and grapes, stopping is also carried out, but this time to encourage fruit formation. The sideshoots, or laterals, are stopped a couple of leaves further on than the flowers so that the plant's energy is spent in producing fruits, not leaves.

All the growths on cucumbers, melons, grape vines, peaches and other plants grown against the sides and roof of the greenhouse should be trained to the wire supports. Overcrowding branches are removed and a well-spaced framework of good stems is retained.

Chrysanthemums have their own complicated stopping programme. The growing points of the shoots are pinched out at various predetermined intervals so that the flush of flowers can be timed almost to the day. Advice on stopping dates can always be obtained from nurseries specializing in chrysanthemums.

Tomato supports – strings strung between two horizontal wires attached to the greenhouse framework by vine eyes

To encourage bushy growth on plants, pinch out the tip of the main shoot

Fuchsia grown as a standard. The growing tip is only pinched out when the stem has reached the required height. This then encourages the bushy head to form

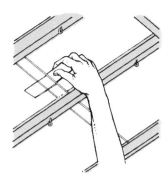

**Clean out dirt that has collected under overlapping panes of glass with a thin metal strip or a plant label**

## Labelling

You may be able to remember the names of many plants in your greenhouse, but the more you have, the more confusing identification may become; particularly if several varieties of one plant are being grown. Clear labelling saves a lot of annoying mix-ups, and the wide variety of tags available means that you should find at least one sort that appeals to you.

Plastic, wooden and metal types are manufactured and should all be inscribed using either a lead or chinagraph pencil, indelible ink, or a permanent felt-tip marker. Never use a ball-point pen, for the writing disappears magically in sunlight. Anodised aluminium labels (the type that are pale grey) can be scrubbed clean if written on in pencil, and used again; plastic ones can also be cleaned in detergent, though they tend to become brittle with age.

I particularly like a new type of label with a plastic window in which the seed packet can be inserted. The information is at your fingertips in a waterproof container.

## Greenhouse hygiene

Growing your plants in a good compost and making sure they are warm and well fed will promote strong and healthy growth, but if the greenhouse is not kept clean, all your good work will be quickly undone. Pests and diseases breed eagerly in soil spilled on paths and gravel, dirty pots stored under the staging and also on dead or dying plants dumped in a corner.

Make a point once a year of giving the entire greenhouse a good clean out. Spring is the best time to do this, for all over wintering pests and their eggs can be destroyed before they emerge. Scrub down the framework inside with a diluted solution of Jeyes' Fluid (wear gloves for it's a smelly job) and wash down the glass both inside and out with water containing detergent. The plants are best moved out of the way during this operation, or stored under the staging.

Dirt always seems to collect where the panes of glass overlap, but it can usually be forced out easily with a strip of thin metal or a plastic label. Wash the staging gravel by placing it in a fine sieve and running a hosepipe over it.

**Algae** The green slime which appears on paths, clay pots and capillary sand and matting is a kind of algae. It is unsightly, smelly and will often hinder plant growth so it must be got rid of. On paths it can be scrubbed off with a stiff brush and elbow grease, but this is a tiring job not to be done more often than you can help. Once cleared, the algae can usually be kept at bay by spraying the path with a chemical called Algofen. This useful substance can also be applied to capillary matting, and even the surface of the soil in seed trays and pots.

On capillary benches containing sand, a substance called Panasand can be mixed with a further quantity of sand which is spread over the surface. The algae is again defeated for a fair length of time.

**Weeds** Weeds can often become a problem under the greenhouse staging but they are easily controlled by applying a herbicide. Clear the ground first by hand or hoe, and then water on a weedkiller such as simazine which will prevent any more emerging. If you are standing plants underneath the staging I would not advise you to use any herbicide. An 8-cm (3-in) layer of gravel will reduce weed growth and provide a good standing ground for the plants.

Never use sodium chlorate to kill weeds in the greenhouse. It is highly inflammable and will also spread sideways in the soil, killing any plants which may be growing in a border outside.

# Greenhouses

If you can afford to heat it a little, your greenhouse can be used throughout the colder months of the year to force many plants into flower or fruit out of their natural season. Here are just a few of the crops which will repay your early care and attention:

## Rhubarb

Dig up a few two- or three-year-old crowns in November and leave them on the surface of the soil for a few days so that the frost gets at them. Then plant them quite close together in 15- or 20-cm (6- or 8-in) deep boxes of peat. Water the crowns well in and cover the boxes with hessian sacks to exclude light. Place them under the greenhouse staging and maintain a temperature of 13° to 16°C (55° to 60°F). Check the boxes every week and water them when they are dry. If you box up a couple of crowns every fortnight in November and December, you will be able to harvest juicy sticks of bright pink rhubarb all through January and February. The crowns will be exhausted after forcing and should be discarded.

**Suitable varieties:** Champagne, Timperley Early.

## French beans

Sow four seeds 2·5cm (1in) deep around the edge of a 15-cm (6-in) pot of John Innes No. 1 potting compost in December, January or February. Water the seeds in and keep the pots in a light position at a constant temperature of 16°C (60°F). Stake the plants with small pieces of brushwood and feed every ten days with a liquid fertilizer when the flowers begin to form. The plants will crop 10 to 12 weeks after being sown and the tender young pods should be picked regularly.

**Suitable varieties:** The Prince, Masterpiece.

## Potatoes

In January, half fill a 20-cm (8-in) pot with John Innes No. 3 potting compost with some extra peat or leafmould added. Plant three sprouted seed potatoes of an early variety 5cm (2in) deep in the compost. Water them well in and place the pot on the greenhouse staging, keeping the temperature around 10°C (50°F). As the shoots grow, gradually topdress with the same compost used for planting, until the pot is almost full. Water thoroughly when the soil shows signs of drying out. The tubers should be ready for harvesting some time in April.

**Suitable varieties:** Epicure, Sharpe's Express.

Sowing French beans in a 15-cm (6-in) pot

Earthing up potatoes in a pot; gradually fill up the pot with compost as the plant grows

Rhubarb crowns to be forced in a box. Sacks will be thrown over to exclude the light

# forcing plants

**Cutting chicons which have been forced in the dark for three weeks**

**Rooting a strawberry runner in a pot. The runner is pegged down to keep the plant firmly in the soil**

### Chicory

At the end of the growing season on the vegetable plot, chicory raised from seed is lifted, all but 2·5cm (1in) of the foliage trimmed off, and the roots stored in sand in a frostproof place. It is these which can be forced to produce succulent, crispy chicons over several months. Pot up three or four of the fleshy roots in a 15-cm (6-in) pot of moist peat and cover this with a box and some sacks, or with black polythene, to keep out the light. In a temperature of 10°C (50°F), thick pointed shoots will appear which will be ready for harvesting in about three weeks. If the smallest amount of light is admitted, the chicons will become yellow and bitter, so do take care to black out properly. Discard the roots after forcing.
**Suitable varieties:** Witloof, Normato.

### Strawberries

Strawberry runners rooted in small pots in June and July are well suited to being forced to produce early fruit. Pot up three well-rooted runners in a 20-cm (8-in) pot of John Innes No. 3 potting compost in August or September. Stand the pots outside for the rest of the year, taking good care to water them if they become dry. In January, bring the pots into the greenhouse and keep them at a temperature of 10°C (50°F). As the plants begin to grow, the temperature can be raised a little until, in February, it hovers around 16°C (60°F). Never let the plants dry out now, and feed them every ten days with a liquid fertilizer when they start to flower. Only allow a

dozen fruits to each plant (pick off the rest) and keep these off the compost with short pieces of cane. You should enjoy mouthwatering fruits in April and May.
**Suitable varieties:** Cambridge Favourite, Royal Sovereign.

### Flowering bulbs

Hyacinths, tulips and narcissi (including daffodils) can all be forced to give early flowers, provided that they are first allowed to establish their root systems. In late August and September, pot the bulbs up close together in containers of compost or bulb fibre so that their 'noses' just protrude. Place the containers outside and cover them with sand or peat. Here the bulbs must remain for at least eight weeks. After this time they can be brought into the greenhouse in successive batches and grown on in a temperature of 13° to 16°C (55° to 60°F).

### Shrubs

Nowadays few people think of forcing shrubs, but if only they knew what could be done with lilac, roses, hydrangeas, deutzia, philadelphus, forsythia, flowering currant and other garden beauties, more of them would be tempted to have a go. The shrubs should be established in large pots for about a year before being forced. Bring them into the greenhouse between November and January, spray them daily with tepid water and give them a temperature of about 10°C (50°F). Copious supplies of water will be needed as the shoots start to grow, and a little more heat will do no harm as the flowers begin to form – up to 16°C (60°F) is enough. When in bloom the plants can be moved into the house. Feed them every ten days during flowering and return them to the greenhouse when they cease to be decorative. They can be lightly pruned and hardened off before being placed outdoors in late spring. Most shrubs will perform better if they are forced every other year.

# Cropping plan

| Crop | February | March | April | May |
|------|----------|-------|-------|-----|
| **TOMATO** <br><br>*Good Varieties* <br>Alicante <br>Moneymaker <br>Ailsa Craig <br>Eurocross BB | If plants are to be grown in greenhouse border, apply a light dressing of well-rotted manure or compost now and dig it in. A good dusting of general fertilizer is also beneficial. | Sow seeds in the middle of the month in pots or boxes of seed compost. Germinate in a temperature of 18°C (64°F) and prick out individually into 8-cm (3-in) pots when large enough to handle. | Keep the plants well supplied with water and remove any sideshoots as they form. Keep the greenhouse temperature between 13° and 16°C (55° and 60°F). | Early in the month plant either in the greenhouse border or in growing bags or large pots of John Innes No. 3. Alternatively use ring culture method. Stake plants at the outset and space 45cm (18in) apart. |
| **CUCUMBER** <br><br>*Good Varieties* <br>Butcher's Disease Resisting <br>Improved Telegraph <br>Femspot  All female <br>Femdan    flowers | Rig up training wires against the glazing bars where the cucumbers are to be positioned. They should run horizontally at 23cm (9in) spacings. | Cucumbers grown in soil borders in the greenhouse are best placed on a mound of manure topped with John Innes No. 3. Make these mounds now 30cm (1ft) high and 45cm (18in) wide. | Sow seeds, two to an 8-cm (3-in) peat pot of seed compost any time this month in a temperature of 18°C (65°F). Remove the weakest seedling after germination. Water the young plants generously. Do not allow to dry out. Temperature: 16°C (60°F). | Plant out, making sure that peat pots are moist, either on mounds, in large pots of John Innes No. 3, or in growing bags. Tie the young plants in to the wire supports. Spray daily with tepid water. |
| **SWEET PEPPER** <br><br>*Good Varieties* <br>New Ace <br>Early Prolific <br>Worldbeater <br>Canape | | Sow seeds in pots or boxes of seed compost and germinate in a temperature of 16°C (60°F). Prick out individually into 8-cm (3-in) pots when large enough to handle. | Pot on into 15- or 20-cm (6- or 8-in) pots of John Innes No. 3 or a soilless equivalent, and keep the greenhouse at a temperature of between 16° and 18°C (60° and 65°F). | Stake the plants with small canes as they develop, and pinch out the growing tips when the plants are about 13cm (5in) high. |
| **AUBERGINE** <br><br>*Good Varieties* <br>Moneymaker <br>Long Purple <br>Black Prince <br>Claresse | Sow seeds in pots or boxes of seed compost and germinate in a temperature of 16°-18°C (60°-65°F). Prick out individually into 8-cm (3-in) pots when large enough to handle, maintaining a temperature of 16°C (60°F). | Water carefully and keep the plants warm. | Pot on into 13-cm (5-in) pots of John Innes No. 2. | Pinch out the growing points when the plants are about 13cm (5in) high. |
| **MELON** <br><br>*Good Varieties* <br>Sweetheart <br>Dutch Net <br>Emerald Gem <br>Charantais | | | Sow seeds in pairs in 8-cm (3-in) peat pots of seed compost and germinate in a temperature of 18°C (65°F). Remove weakest seedling after germination and maintain temperature at 16°C (60°F). | Plant the young melons either in growing bags or on mounds of John Innes No. 3 on staging or borders. Equip each plant with a cane to take its growth up to the training wires. |

Many vegetables can be raised in the greenhouse, pricked out into seed trays and hardened off before being planted in the vegetable plot. Seed packets provide valuable information on sowing times for individual varieties.

| June | July | August | September | October |
|---|---|---|---|---|
| Water carefully. Remove sideshoots continually and tie in the stem as it grows. Feed plants as soon as first flowers open. Assist fruit setting by spraying with tepid water. | Keep an eye open for greenfly and whitefly and spray if troublesome. Continue feeding at weekly intervals. Harvest fruits regularly as soon as ripe. | Stop the plants when five or six trusses of fruit have been formed. Keep removing sideshoots. Check for pests and diseases and combat when necessary. Carry on feeding. | Stop feeding and allow the plants a little less water to hasten fruit ripening. | Pick any fruits which are not ripe and store them indoors. Dig the plants up and consign them to the compost heap. |
| To prevent fruits from tasting bitter remove all male flowers (those with very short stalks) before they open. All-female varieties will not carry any. Tie in shoots to wires. Stop sideshoots after two leaves have formed. Feed weekly. | First fruits can be picked this month as soon as ripe. Shade the house with blinds or whitewash. Topdress plants when roots appear above compost. | Whitefly is a problem on cucumbers. Spray to control it as soon as it is seen. The same applies to red spider mite, though a moist atmosphere can keep this pest at bay. | Harvest the last fruits this month and clear out the plants and their compost. | |
| Spray the flowers with tepid water as they open so that the fruit is set. Feed every week with liquid fertilizer. | Keep an eye open for greenfly and whitefly and spray if they become a problem. | Harvest the fruits when green and plump. If they are allowed to turn red they are still edible but the plant will start to slow down as its fruits are ripening. | Continue harvesting and feeding. | Remove any fruit still on the plant and use them if they are large enough. Discard the plants. |
| Pot on into their final pots, 20cm (8in) in diameter. Use John Innes No. 3 or a soilless equivalent. Spray plants against red spider mite and whitefly if these are a problem. | Spray the flowers as they open with tepid water to encourage the fruit to set. Feed every two weeks with liquid fertilizer. Allow only six or eight fruits per plant. | Harvest the fruits when large enough and while they are still shiny. If allowed to become dull they lose their flavour and are tough. Pinch out all sideshoots to keep the plant's shape. | Continue harvesting and feeding. Discard plants when all fruit has been picked. | |
| Tie in stems to wires. Pinch out sideshoots when two leaves have formed. Allow only 4 or 5 fruits per plant. Remove a male flower and use it to pollinate all 4 female flowers on same day. Spray foliage with tepid water daily. | Feed with liquid fertilizer every 10 days after fruits have set. Stop main stem when it reaches ridge of house. Topdress mound when roots appear above compost. | As melons swell they become heavy so support them in net bags hung from wires. When fruits start to smell ripe, cut down on watering to prevent them splitting. Pick when ready. | Continue harvesting. Discard plants and clear away mounds when all fruit has been gathered. | |

41

# Cropping plan

| Symbols | |
|---|---|
| 20° | Sow in this temperature °C. |
| | Prick out into boxes. |
| 4" | Pot into this size pot. |
| | Take cuttings. |
| 13° | Bring into green-house at this temperature °C. |
| | Plunge outdoors in sand or peat. |
| | Flowering season. |
| | Berrying season. |

| Plant | Description |
|---|---|
| Begonia semperflorens | Glossy green or brown leaves and small pink, white or red flowers carried in large numbers. |
| Beloperone (Shrimp Plant) | Small green leaves and pink bracts which look vaguely like shrimps. |
| Calceolaria hybrids (Slipper Flower) | Red, yellow and white pouches, often spotted with a darker colour, are carried over a mound of green leaves |
| Campanula medium (Canterbury Bell) | Large pink, white or blue bells carried on long stems. |
| Capsicum annuum (Ornamental Pepper) | Pointed red, cream and purple berries and small green leaves. |
| Celosia plumosa (Prince of Wales' Feathers) | Feathery plumes of red, orange or yellow, carried above fresh green leaves. |
| Cineraria | Red, blue, white or pink daisy flowers carried in a round head over large green leaves. |
| Cleome spinosa (Spider flower) | Fingered green leaves on a tall stem topped with spiky pink flowers. |
| Coleus hybrids (Flame nettle) | Brilliantly coloured leaves which are attractive the whole year round. |
| Crocus (Dutch hybrids) | Blue, white and yellow cup-shaped flowers held among grassy leaves. |
| Cyclamen hybrids | White, pink, magenta, salmon and red reflexed flowers held over attractive marbled leaves. |
| Fuchsia | Pendant flowers in many colours carried on arching stems. Can be trained as standards on a single stem. |
| Heliotrope | Pale purple, sweetly-scented flowers and green leaves. Can be trained as standards on a single stem. |
| Hyacinth (Dutch hybrids) | Large scented heads of flower which may be red, pink, yellow, white or blue. |
| Impatiens (Busy Lizzie) | Red, white, orange or pink flowers and green, maroon or variegated leaves. |
| Kalanchoe | Glossy green leaves and many tiny red flowers carried in dense heads. |
| Lobelia | Trailing green stems covered with white, blue or carmine flowers. |
| Narcissus hybrids (including daffodils) | White, yellow and orange flowers with large or small trumpets and grassy leaves. |
| Pelargonium ($F_1$ hybrids) (Geraniums) | Red, pink or white flowers and downy green leaves often banded with brown. |
| Primula obconica | White, pink, orange or magenta flowers over green leaves. The leaves bring some people out in a rash. |
| Schizanthus (Poor Man's Orchid) | Multicoloured flowers held over ferny green leaves. |
| Stock (Beauty of Nice) | Sweetly scented pink, white, magenta or cream flowers carried in spikes. |
| Tulip hybrids | White, red, orange, yellow, dark brown or multi-coloured cup-shaped flowers held over broad leaves. |
| Zygocactus (Christmas cactus) | Flat, glossy green stems and cerise, starry flowers. |

| Jan | Feb | Mar | Apr | May | Jun | Jul | Aug | Sep | Oct | Nov | Dec |
|-----|-----|-----|-----|-----|-----|-----|-----|-----|-----|-----|-----|

# Garden Frames

As an extension of the greenhouse, or as a feature on its own, a cold or heated frame is a relatively cheap and quite versatile piece of equipment which can be put to many uses in the garden: new plants can be raised; frost-tender ones can be given protection or overwintered; vegetables and fruits can be grown to crop out of season, and greenhouse-grown plants can be hardened off before being transferred to the garden.

There are lots of designs to choose from, but the main things to look for are effective insulation and good light transmission. Remember too to pick a frame deep enough to accommodate the plants you want to grow.

If you are unimpressed by what you see offered for sale, make a garden frame yourself; old timber can form the sides and an unwanted window frame or some plastic sheeting the lid or 'light'.

## Dutch type

The strong wooden sides and large area of glass in this single-span frame make it both well insulated and well lit. This might be a frame to avoid if children play anywhere near, for they could be badly injured if they fell on to it. The glass is rather expensive to replace as well (it measures about 1·5m by 75cm (5 by 2½ft)).

**Dutch-type frame**

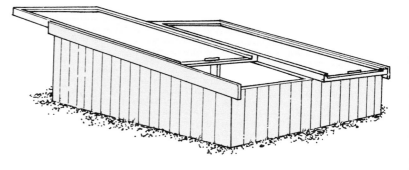

**Home-made box frame**

## Home-made box

This is one of the simplest types of garden frame which can be knocked together at home. Treat the timber with a wood preservative other than creosote, which is toxic to plants, and use brass screws to assemble the sides. The back of the 'light' can be hinged to allow access.

## Rigid plastic

This 'double-span' shaped plastic frame has transparent sliding panels which are corrugated and so quite strong. It is anchored to the ground by metal pegs and offers sufficient height in the centre for moderately tall plants. Remember that plastics, whether rigid or flexible, have a limited life in the garden and will eventually become weak and brittle; they also insulate less efficiently than glass and admit less light.

**Rigid plastic frame**

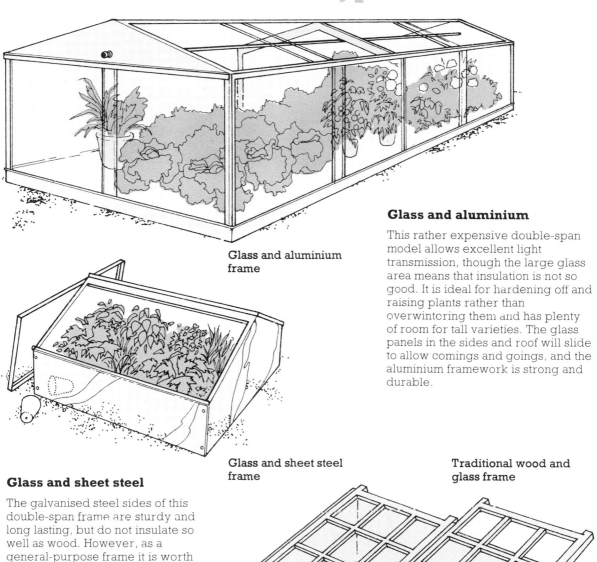

**Glass and aluminium frame**

## Glass and aluminium

This rather expensive double-span model allows excellent light transmission, though the large glass area means that insulation is not so good. It is ideal for hardening off and raising plants rather than overwintering them and has plenty of room for tall varieties. The glass panels in the sides and roof will slide to allow comings and goings, and the aluminium framework is strong and durable.

**Glass and sheet steel frame**

**Traditional wood and glass frame**

## Glass and sheet steel

The galvanised steel sides of this double-span frame are sturdy and long lasting, but do not insulate so well as wood. However, as a general-purpose frame it is worth having, for it can usually be bought quite cheaply and will keep many spring-raised crops warm enough.

## Traditional wood and glass

The old-fashioned English single-span 'cold frame' can still be bought and has many good points. It is large, allows in plenty of light, its wood or brick sides keep in the heat, and it can be expected to have a long life. Its only real disadvantage is that the lights are heavy and rather difficult to manoeuvre.

# Garden Frames

Smaller and cheaper than a greenhouse it may be, but a garden frame still needs to be given a good spot in the garden if it is to do its job properly. It follows that the recommendations given for putting up a greenhouse (see pp.12-13) apply to some extent to the garden frame, but here they can be a little more flexible.

As with the greenhouse, light and heat are major considerations, but with the frame, its accessibility should be its strong point. If it is to be used in conjunction with the greenhouse it must be fairly near to it to prevent you from staggering half a mile with boxes and pots of plants which are to be grown on or hardened off.

Single-span frames (which have lights that slope one way only) can very easily be positioned along the south side of a greenhouse and can even be joined to it. Here they will get the maximum light available, good insulation, and they can also make use of greenhouse facilities for heating (see p.00). Though a single-span frame should face south, the double-span (which slopes both ways from a central ridge) can run in any direction provided that it is in a well-lit spot.

Make sure that there is a gravel or concrete path of a good width around your frame if it is a large and permanent fixture. Smaller models may only be in use for a few months of the year, or you may wish to move them, so such provision is unnecessary.

**Permanent double-span frame with a path of flags round the outside to ensure easy access in all weathers**

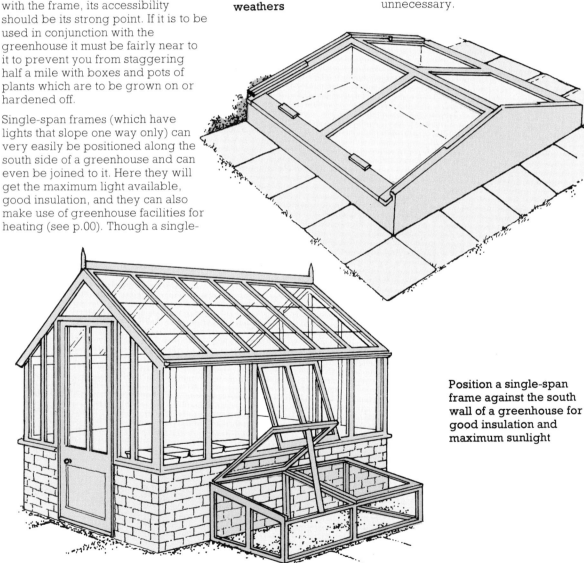

**Position a single-span frame against the south wall of a greenhouse for good insulation and maximum sunlight**

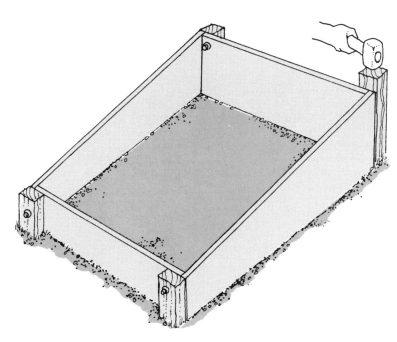

Hold a frame firmly on the ground by bolting it to long wooden stakes driven into the soil

usually positioned in one place permanently, and a concrete or brick foundation must be constructed in exactly the same way as for a greenhouse (see p.12). Levelling is very important for the double-span types. If the foundations are uneven, the lights will stick and be difficult to open and close.

As with greenhouses, some manufacturers supply precast concrete foundations which can save you a lot of time and energy. The frames are simply bolted to the concrete kerbs which are laid on level ground.

## Preservatives

Aluminium frames, like aluminium greenhouses, need no form of protection, but English frames, and others made of timber, can be coated with primer and then green or white gloss paint.

Dutch frames are seldom painted but are usually coated with a preservative such as copper naphthenate, either the green or brown variety. Creosote is toxic to plants and so should never be used. Check and renew the preservative on all frames every few years when it starts to wear off.

## Putting the frame together

Most small frames will be in one piece anyway, but larger models should be bolted or screwed together on top of the foundations, and the lights added last. Glazing might involve puttying or the use of clips – whichever is the case, make sure that the glass does not slip. You will be lifting the lights up frequently, and sliding sheets of sharp-edged glass can cause considerable damage when they come into contact with skin.

Manufacturers can nearly always be relied upon to give good advice on putting up their own brand of frame, and written instructions of varying lucidity are usually provided.

## Foundations

Small pre-fabricated garden frames need no foundations at all, unless manufacturers specify otherwise. Their portability is one of their advantages and any permanent anchorage would make them less versatile. Some of them are equipped with metal pegs which will hold them firm temporarily, and those which are not can be screwed or bolted to 45cm (18in) long wooden stakes driven into the ground. A garden frame does not offer as much wind resistance as a greenhouse, but it is lighter and can still fly away in a sharp gust of wind if not securely pinned down.

Larger frames such as the Dutch and English models, and the double-span aluminium and glass type, are

# Garden Frames

## Soil or gravel?

What you do with the piece of ground inside the frame will depend entirely on the plants you want to grow.

**Crops in the soil** Delicious early pickings of lettuce, carrots and many other vegetables can be raised in a garden frame, and provided that the existing soil is in a reasonable condition there is no reason why it cannot be retained. It is always a good idea to enrich it a little though, and a bucketful of well-rotted manure or garden compost, or even coarse peat, dug into each square yard, together with three or four handfuls of a general fertilizer such as blood, bone and fish meal, will provide just the right conditions to keep most plants happy.

Tread the soil to firm it and then rake it level. Now you should have a nourishing piece of ground ready to receive seeds or plants. For continued success, repeat this treatment every year, and in any case, give the dusting of fertilizer before every crop goes in. If your ground is heavy, stony or otherwise unsuitable, you would do well to remove it to a depth of a foot or so and replace it with good topsoil.

When the frame is empty, leave the lights off so that the weather can get in to soak the soil and wash away any impurities. If this is not possible, try to give the soil at least one really good flooding with a hosepipe every year.

**Pots and boxes** If plants in pots and boxes are to occupy the frame, it is best to spread an 8-cm (3-in) layer of gravel or weathered ashes over the soil. If this is not done, worms will find their way into the containers causing drainage problems, and weeds will also make a nuisance of themselves. Where frames are positioned on patios and roofs, no drainage material is necessary.

**If plants in pots and boxes are to fill your frame, dig out the soil and fill the base with a 8-cm (3-in) layer of gravel or weathered ashes**

**If crops are to be sown directly into the soil in the frame it must be dug over and enriched every year**

## Heating

If you can equip your frame with heating apparatus, its versatility will be greatly improved. Tender plants can be relied upon to survive the winter, and early vegetables will be ready that much sooner in spring.

**Warming cables** Electric warming cables are the most satisfactory means of heating for they take up little room, need no maintenance and are inexpensive to run. Lay them out 8 to 10cm (3 to 4in) below the surface of the soil where plants are being grown direct in the ground – manufacturers will advise on the amount of cable needed in a given area and how close it should be

Heating the frame with space-heating cables round the walls and soil-warming cables 15-cm (6-in) under the soil. The rod thermostats ensure that the temperature remains steady

spaced. Added protection can be given by fixing warming cable to the inside walls of the frame above soil level.

If the frame is sited next to the greenhouse it will be a simple matter to run the cable through the wall to the existing supply; if it is not, consult a professional electrician who will advise on connecting the cables to your domestic circuit.

Always use a thermostat with this system. It will save you a lot of money.

**Heating pipes** If the frame is alongside a greenhouse heated with hot-water pipes, a single or double row of pipes can be taken through it.

A plumber will advise you on the possibility of enlarging your greenhouse heating system to cope with the needs of a frame.

**Paraffin heaters** Though it is not always satisfactory in the confined space of a frame, a greenhouse paraffin heater can be used if there is no alternative.

Consult the manufacturers' literature to find a heater which will be large or small enough for your frame, and make sure that it is provided with firm standing ground and a little ventilation at all times. In frames which lack depth you may have to excavate a hole to take the heater, and this should be wide enough to allow a free passage of air to the burner.

## Insulation

Keeping the heat in your frame means keeping some money in your pocket. Insulation is a simple and unsophisticated task here, for hessian sheets or sacks thrown over frames at night will retain a fair amount of the warmth built up during the day. If you are a perfectionist or do not possess any sacking, you can buy special mats fitted with eyelets which allow them to be tied over the frame.

Alternative methods of retaining heat include double glazing with polythene, and surrounding the walls of the frame with a mattress of straw sandwiched between two layers of chicken wire.

**Above:** Cover the frame with sacking on cold nights
**Right:** More permanent insulation is given by surrounding the frame with a straw mattress

# Garden Frames

## Ventilation

Lowering the temperature in a garden frame poses few problems. In a greenhouse, cooling air can only be admitted through ventilators and doors, but the frame can usually be entirely stripped of its lights so that fresh air circulates freely around the plants.

This is the best thing to do in the heart of summer – take the lights off completely and stack them in a convenient place on a level base, tying them down so that they will not lift in sharp gusts of wind. Through the rest of the year a more subtle means of ventilation is needed. Lights which slide can simply be pulled down a little to allow the required amount of ventilation – either a crack or a large gap. If the weather is nippy, but you feel a little fresh air is needed, pull down every other light just an inch or two.

Alternatively – and this method must be used on lights which are hinged to the frame at the back – prop them open with blocks of wood. An effective prop can be made from a piece of old floorboarding measuring about 15 by 30cm (6 by 12in). Cut a couple of 'steps' in the wood and it can be used to hold the frame open at various heights. Some firms fit their frames with casement stays which vary in their degree of sophistication. Provided that they hold the lights firmly they are worth having.

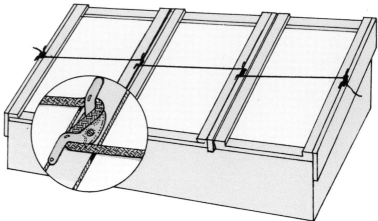

**Secure the lights in windy weather by tying them down with a rope wound round cleats**

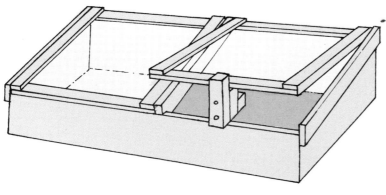

**This easily made wooden block will prop the light open by varying amounts to allow ventilation in warm weather**

Always make sure that the lights are securely fastened to the frames in windy weather. Heavy pieces of timber or ropes strung between cleats will usually hold them down.

## Shading

During spring, when melons, ridge cucumbers and other tender morsels are developing nicely in a garden frame, a sharp burst of bright sunshine can scorch the leaves and set the plants back severely. A well-diluted application of a whitewash compound such as Coolglass (see p.19) will diffuse harmful rays, while still admitting enough light to keep the plants growing.

Muslin or scrim is occasionally sold as a shading material and it can be thrown over the frame and weighted, or attached to a wooden framework. Green plastic close-weave netting is a more permanent alternative, and this can be rolled up at one end of the frame and pulled over the lights whenever the sun shines brightly. Lath or bamboo blinds are just as effective but their cost might deter you from investing in them.

## Watering

It is a simple job to water plants in a small garden frame with a watering can or hosepipe fitted with a rose, but in long runs of Dutch or English-type frames, some system of semi-automatic watering is a great time saver.

**Perforated hose** Several types of perforated hose are manufactured which can be laid along the ground, in this case between the plants in the frame, and connected up to a water tap. When the supply is turned on, water is emitted from the pipe in small jets and at varying angles.

**Overhead spray lines** Instead of being laid on the ground, this system is suspended over the plants. The pipes are usually made from rigid alkathene tubing, and coarse spray nozzles are fitted at intervals of 1·25 to 2m (4 to 6ft).

The disadvantage of using both these systems with pot plants is that all of them are watered at once, regardless of the state of the compost. However, many healthy plants have been raised in this way so it can't be all that bad.

**Above:** One method of watering in the frame is with a perforated hose
**Below:** Sit pots on a bed of moist sand for plants to take up water by capillarity

**Capillary watering** The system of capillary watering (see p.23) is not just something for the greenhouse; it can be modified a little and used to good effect in a garden frame. In this situation it is better to revert to sand, for it is easier to handle outdoors than capillary matting and will be cheaper when used over a large area.

Make the soil in the frame level and quite firm, and lay a sheet of heavy gauge polythene over it. Spread a 5-cm (2-in) layer of coarse river sand over the polythene and smooth and level this too. Water is applied by a trickle irrigation line which can be snaked in between the plants so that it moistens the entire sand area. Remember to use only plastic pots with several holes in the base, or to supply clay pots with a wick.

The trickle line can also be used on its own when plants are growing in soil in the frame. Switch it on at the tap whenever the soil starts to dry out.

Whatever system you decide on, you can still cash in on any light shower of rain by pulling down the frame lights for an hour or two.

# Garden Frames

The only thing that stops a garden frame from doing everything a greenhouse can is its size. Apart from that one difference it is as versatile as its larger relation.

Just as in a greenhouse, seeds can be raised in pots and boxes if a little heat is given. Cuttings can be rooted in containers too, or they can be dibbed into a mixture of peat and sand laid in the frame itself. Half-ripe cuttings (see p.32) are especially at home for they may be dibbed into the frame in summer and left there through winter under the protection of the lights.

If you want to use your frame as a means of ensuring food or flower crops right through the year the cropping plans on pages 40 to 42 will give you a few ideas. Either on its own or as a satellite of the greenhouse, the frame is particularly suited to hardening off plants in spring and to getting the more tender ones through the winter unscathed.

## Hardening off

Young plants raised from seeds and cuttings in a greenhouse or frame should not be unceremoniously transferred to the garden without first being accustomed to the rigours of their new environment. A short spell of hardening off, as it is called, will prepare them for an ordeal that might otherwise cause their growth to be severely checked. Sturdy young vegetable and bedding plants need hardening off if they have been raised in a greenhouse, but the process is very simple and need take only a couple of weeks if the weather is reasonable.

**Harden off plants by moving them from the greenhouse to the frame before setting them outside**

Place the plants in the frame during spring; or if they have been raised in the frame, reduce or turn off the heat. Ventilate the frame during the first week from morning till evening, closing it down again each night. Open it a little wider every day. During the second week the light can be left open a little at night, until towards the end of the week it is removed completely or opened to its full extent. Plants which are frost tender should not be uncovered completely at night until the danger of sub-zero temperatures is past.

After this short period of acclimatization the plants should take quite readily to life in the open air.

**Chop back pelargoniums and box them up before overwintering them in the frame**

**Boxed-up chrysanthemum stools overwintered in the frame. They can be used as a source of cuttings in the spring**

## Overwintering

If you don't plan to grow food crops in your frame through the winter it can act as a depository for flowering plants which need some form of protection from the cruel weather. In housing these it will also take some of the strain off the greenhouse which is probably full to bursting with plants of a similar disposition.

Pelargoniums can be lifted from the garden, chopped back a little and boxed up in compost before being overwintered in a frame given sufficient heat to keep out frost. Chrysanthemums which have been cut down to a few inches of stem (making them into what are known as 'stools') can be treated in a similar way, though an unheated frame will suit them fine. If you can heat the frame a little in spring you will be able to take cuttings from your chrysanths without having to transfer them to the greenhouse.

In addition to these plants, any which are described as being not entirely hardy in British winters can be given a home in the frame from November to March. Planted in pots or boxes, or straight into the soil, they will stand a good chance of survival even in an unheated frame.

# Garden Frames

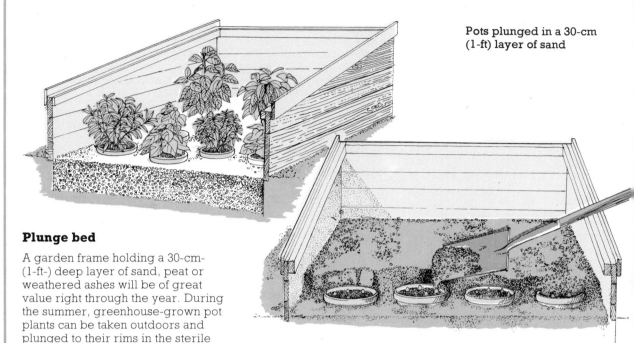

Pots plunged in a 30-cm (1-ft) layer of sand

## Plunge bed

A garden frame holding a 30-cm-(1-ft-) deep layer of sand, peat or weathered ashes will be of great value right through the year. During the summer, greenhouse-grown pot plants can be taken outdoors and plunged to their rims in the sterile medium which will prevent their roots from drying out too rapidly. Extra space is gained in the greenhouse for crops such as tomatoes, cucumbers and melons, and the pot plants will develop into sturdy specimens as a result of their summer excursion.

Nearly all alpine and rock plants grown in pots will appreciate the cooler, moister environment as soon as they have finished flowering – from spring onwards.

Though the lights are not used during summer, in autumn and winter they will be needed for then comes the bulb-forcing season. After being potted up, all bulbs need a period of about eight weeks in which to form their roots, and they are most happy to do this when plunged in a cool, slightly moist medium. This time the pots are not just sunk to their rims, they are entirely covered. The lights are not needed to increase the temperature at all, but they should be placed over the frame to keep out heavy rain or the pots will become waterlogged. Always prop the lights open a little to allow ventilation, and on no account turn the heating on.

## Hotbed

The hotbed is a primitive but effective means of making your own propagating frame if no heating apparatus is available. Build up a heap of fresh strawy stable manure (or stable manure and leaves in equal parts) and tread it down so that it has a flat top. The heap should be 60cm to 1m (2 to 3ft) deep and large enough to hold a portable garden frame. Make sure that the straw is quite moist when you are making the heap – have a watering can ready to drench any dry bits.

Plunged pots of bulbs being covered with peat

Frame positioned on a hotbed. The pots are plunged into a layer of sand and the soil thermometer records the temperature

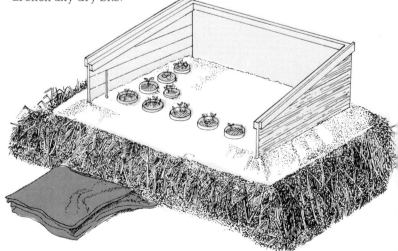

On top of the manure spread a 15-cm (6-in) layer of seed or cutting compost or coarse sand; the former if seeds or cuttings are to be put directly into the frame and the latter if they are to be put in pots which will then be plunged to their rims. Position the frame on top next, and inside it stick a soil thermometer which will indicate the temperature of the hotbed.

As the bacteria get to work on breaking down the manure a lot of heat will be generated and it is this that the gardener can make use of.

The temperature of the heap will rise dramatically over the first few days but will then drop a little until it remains steady. This is the time when seeds and cuttings can be put into the frame.

Make your hotbed in spring so that when its heating power begins to die down – after a couple of months – the sun will be strong enough to take over. Remember to cover the light with sacking or a piece of old carpet at night to keep in the heat which will otherwise be rapidly lost.

## Cropping Plan

### Flowers from your frame

### January

Remove further batches of plunged bulbs to bring into flower. August-planted freesias in flower – bring indoors in pots or use as cut blooms.

### February

Anemones in bloom from October planting – cut flowers for indoor decoration. Take cuttings from chrysanthemums overwintering in heated frame. Remove further batches of plunged bulbs to bring into flower. September-planted freesias in flower. Transfer Beauty of Nice and East Lothian Stocks to greenhouse for flowering.

### MARCH

Leave anemones undisturbed after flowering. Sow bedding plants in pots and boxes in heated frame. Continue to take chrysanthemum cuttings. Take cuttings from fuchsias and pelargoniums overwintering in heated frame. Box up dahlia tubers in potting compost and place in heated frame.

### April

Continue to take pelargonium and fuchsia cuttings. Move bedding plants from greenhouse to frame to harden off. Take hydrangeas into greenhouse and start into growth. Take cuttings from dahlias.

### May

Bring alpines and rock plants from greenhouse into plunge bed. Harden off bedding plants prior to planting out. Root softwood cuttings in heated frame.

### June

Plunge cinerarias, calceolarias, azaleas, cyclamen, hydrangeas, primulas, solanums and other pot plants in frame. Root more softwood cuttings.

### July

Pot plants and alpines still in plunge bed. Root semi-ripe cuttings in frame.

### August

Pot plants and alpines still in plunge bed. Root more semi-ripe cuttings. Pot up freesia corms and place in frame which can be kept frost-free.

### September

Return plunged pot plants and alpines to greenhouse. Plunge daffodils, narcissi, tulips and hyacinths for Christmas flowering. Box up pelargoniums and chrysanthemums and place in frame to overwinter. Place tender fuchsias in frame. Pot up further batch of freesias.

### October

Plant Anemone St Brigid and De Caen types in unheated frame. Place Beauty of Nice and East Lothian stocks in frame to overwinter before flowering in spring. Plunge more bulbs for succession. Store dahlia tubers in boxes of dry peat in frostproof frame after removing frosted foliage.

### November

Take out bulbs plunged in September for Christmas flowering and move to house or greenhouse. Plunge more bulbs for succession.

### December

Remove further batches of plunged bulbs to bring into flower. Plunge more bulbs for succession.

# Frame cropping programme

## Vegetables Through The Year

The frame is a great asset to any gardener keen on vegetable growing.

Try some of the crops listed here and increase the variety of food on your table.

## Beetroot

*Varieties:* Boltardy, Early Bunch.
*Sow:* February. Unheated frame. 2·5cm (1in) deep in rows 23cm (9in) apart. Good but not freshly manured soil.
*Thin:* to 10cm (4in) apart when large enough to handle.
*Cultivation:* Ventilate gradually until lights are left off completely from April onwards. Water and weed when necessary.
*Harvest:* June-July when size of a tennis ball.

## Carrots

*Varieties:* Amstel, Early Nantes.
*Sow:* Mid-January in temperature of 10°C (50°F), February if unheated. Thinly 0·5cm (¼in) deep in rows 23cm (9in) apart. Well-worked but not freshly manured soil.
*Cultivation:* Ventilate during bright sunshine. Water and weed when necessary. Remove lights in April.
*Harvest:* Mid-April to late May. Young carrots pulled when large enough to eat which is why thinning is not needed.

## Cucumber

*Varieties:* Butcher's Disease Resisting, Improved Telegraph.
*Sow:* Mid-March in peat pots in greenhouse. Temperature: 18°C (65°F).
*Transplant:* to heated frame in Mid-April. Temperature: 18°-21°C (65°-70°F). Mound of rich, well-manured soil. One plant is sufficient for a frame 2 by 1·25m (6 by 4ft).

*Cultivation:* Pinch plant when six leaves have formed. Peg down four sideshoots and train towards corners of frame and then pinch these also. Spray with water daily. Remove male flowers before they open or fruits will taste bitter. Pinch out shoots just beyond developing female flowers. Water well when necessary. Topdress with compost later in season when white roots appear. Ventilate gently during warm weather, more generously in summer, but keep lights on at night. Shade from May onwards in bright sun. Give liquid feed weekly. Keep fruits off soil.
*Harvest:* July-August. Cut regularly.

## Endive

*Varieties:* Winter Lettuce-leaved, Batavian Green.
*Sow:* Mid-August in light, well-cultivated, well-fertilized soil. Thinly 1cm (½in) deep in rows 30cm (1ft) apart.
*Thin:* to leave 23cm (9in) apart.
*Cultivation:* Cover with lights from mid-October onwards but ventilate when warm during day. Weed and water when necessary. When well hearted throw sacks or carpet over frame to completely exclude light and blanch leaves.
*Harvest:* About six weeks after starting to blanch; December-March.

## French beans

*Varieties:* The Prince, Tendergreen.
*Sow:* Mid-March, 2·5cm (1in) deep, 10cm (4in) apart in rows 30cm (1ft) apart. Well-manured, well-cultivated soil. Cover with lights.
*Cultivation:* Ventilate when weather is warm or sun is bright. Remove lights in late May. Water and weed as necessary. Spray with tepid water when flowers

open. Stake with twiggy branches if plants flop. Apply liquid feed weekly.
*Harvest:* June-July. Pick regularly.

## Lettuce

*Varieties and sowing dates:* Kwiek: August-September; Kloek: October; May Queen: October-March.
*Sow:* Thinly 0·5cm (¼in) deep in rows 30cm (1ft) apart. Rich, well-cultivated soil. Lights in place October onwards.
*Thin:* to leave 23cm (9in) apart.
*Cultivation:* Ventilate and weed when necessary. Water sparingly as required.
*Harvest:* Kwiek: November-December; Kloek: February-March; May Queen: March-June.

## Marrow and courgette

*Varieties:* Green Bush, Zucchini.
*Sow:* March in greenhouse at temperature of 16°C (60°F). Singly in peat pots.
*Transplant:* to mound of well-manured soil in cold frame during mid-April. Two plants will fit in a 2 by 1·25m (6 by 4ft) frame.
*Cultivation:* Give an adequate supply of water at all times. Ventilate and weed when necessary. Apply liquid feed weekly from May onwards. Hand pollinate flowers. Remove light altogether in mid-May.
*Harvest:* Late June/early July onwards. Cut Zucchini regularly as courgettes or leave to grow into marrows.

## Melon

*Varieties:* Sweetheart, Ogen.
*Sow, Transplant* and *Train* as for cucumbers. Fruits will be carried on secondary sideshoots which arise from the four shoots trained to the corners.
*Cultivation:* Hand pollinate half a dozen flowers at same time. If they set remove all others.

Reduce number of swelling fruits to four when they can be seen to have set. Water well and feed every week. Trim off excessive growth. Reduce water supply considerably when fruits start to smell ripe.
*Harvest:* July to mid-September. Cut when end of fruit furthest from stalk begins to feel soft.

### Radish

*Varieties:* French Breakfast, Cherry Belle.

*Sow:* Early February-March in unheated frame with rich soil. Thinly 1cm (½in) deep in rows 10cm (4in) apart or between other crops such as lettuce and turnips.
*Cultivation:* Ventilate and water when necessary. Should grow quickly and mature before the crops they are sown with.
*Harvesting:* April onwards as soon as of an edible size. Do not leave too long or they will become woody.

### Turnip

*Varieties:* White Milan, Jersey Navet.
*Sow:* Late February-March in unheated frame with rich soil. Thinly 1cm (½in) deep in rows 30cm (1ft) apart.
*Thin:* to leave 10cm (4in) apart.
*Cultivation:* Water and weed when necessary. Ventilate freely on bright days. Remove lights completely in late April.
*Harvest:* June onwards when the size of golf balls as then they are most tender.

## Frame cropping programme

The suggestions given here will help you plan a year's cropping in your frame. Any crops which occupy the same months can be interchanged, e.g. melons with cucumbers. Either devote your whole frame to one programme or divide it into sections using a different programme for each.

| | | Jan | Feb | Mar | Apr | May | Jun | Jul | Aug | Sep | Oct | Nov | Dec |
|---|---|---|---|---|---|---|---|---|---|---|---|---|---|
| 1 | | | Carrots | | | | | | | | | | |
| | | | | | | Melon | | | | | | | |
| | | | | | | | | | | | Lettuce: Kwiek | | |
| 2 | | Vegetables for outdoor planting | | | | | | | | | | | |
| | | | | | French beans | | | | | | | | |
| | | Endive (cont) | | | | | | | Endive | | | | |
| 3 | | | | Turnips intercropped with radishes | | | | | | | | | |
| | | Lettuce: Kloek (cont) | | | | | | | | | Lettuce: Kloek | | |
| 4 | | Vegetables for outdoor planting | | | | | | | | | | | |
| | | | | | | Marrow | | | | | | | |
| | | Lettuce: May Queen (cont) | | | | | | | | | Lettuce: May Queen | | |
| 5 | | | | Beetroot | | | | | | | | | |
| | | Endive (cont) | | | | | | | Endive | | | | |
| 6 | | Vegetables for outdoor planting | | | | | | | | | | | |
| | | | | | | Cucumber | | | | | | | |
| | | | | | | | | | | | Lettuce: Kwiek | | |

# Cloches

Several centuries ago the French were using small glass domes or 'bell jars' to protect plants in the open during the colder months of the year. These never really caught on in Britain, but a variation on them, the cloche, took not only the French word for 'bell' as its name, but also their place on this country's vegetable plots.

Any good cloche should have these features:

**Strength** The ability to withstand being moved around is important, as is a resistance to wind. Glass is rigid but brittle; plastic supple but not so long lived.

**Ease of erection** Several types of wire support may look complicated, but once the technique has been mastered they are not difficult to put together. Avoid those with flimsy clips though which buckle or break.

**Good light transmission** Both glass- and plastic-covered cloches will admit plenty of light but avoid those with bulky framework.

**Portability** The great advantage of cloches should be their ease of mobility. Pick a type which you can move around without giving yourself a hernia.

**Ventilation** All cloches should have ventilation facilities, whether this involves propping up the sides with a brick or adjusting panes of glass.

## Types and Designs

**Glass barn** Both high- and low-sided variations of this model are available. It offers plenty of room for one row of larger crops, or for two rows of more modest-sized vegetables. The weight of the cloche is usually sufficient to hold it firm in windy weather (provided no gaps are left) and one roof pane is adjustable to allow ventilation.

**Glass or plastic barn with netting** This variation on the barn cloche has several useful features. It can be clad with glass or plastic, has a carrying handle, a rigid wire frame, and is covered with plastic netting. This means that when the glass or plastic sheets are removed the cloche can be left in position to provide protection against birds.

**Glass tent** Tent cloches are cheaper than barn types (there is less glass in them) and are fine for smaller-sized crops. The two panes of glass may be held together by wire supports or by simple clips – the 'Rumsey Clip' is shown here.

(1) **Glass barn cloche**
(2) **Barn cloches with handle and netting**
(3) **Glass tent cloche**

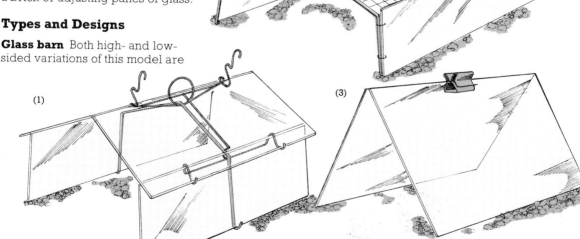

(1)

(2)

(3)

**Polythene tent and barn** A simple wire framework holds polythene sheeting in a barn or tent shape. These cloches are relatively cheap but they retain heat less efficiently than their glass counterparts and the polythene will fall to pieces after a couple of years. Being light they need to be fastened down all the time.

**Rigid plastic tunnel** The midway stage between polythene and glass, rigid plastic has the advantage of being light yet strong but it will turn brittle and will eventually need renewing. Five to ten years is roughly its useful life. Some types of rigid plastic cloche are sold ready moulded, others are bent over stiff wire supports which are pushed into the ground, and some have sliding panels to allow cultivation and ventilation.

**Polythene tunnel** This is the cheapest type of continuous cloche and is very easy to make. The polythene can be lifted back for cultivation and ventilation and is cheap to renew every two years or so.

## End pieces

All continuous cloches, apart from polythene tunnels which are tied down, should be fitted with closely fitting end pieces. Some manufacturers supply these for their own cloches, but a sheet of glass will do the job just as well on other models if it is held firmly against the end with a strong stake. If no end piece is fitted, strong winds may lift and damage the cloches, and animals may find their way in to eat or sleep on the crop.

Polythene and wire tent and barn cloches

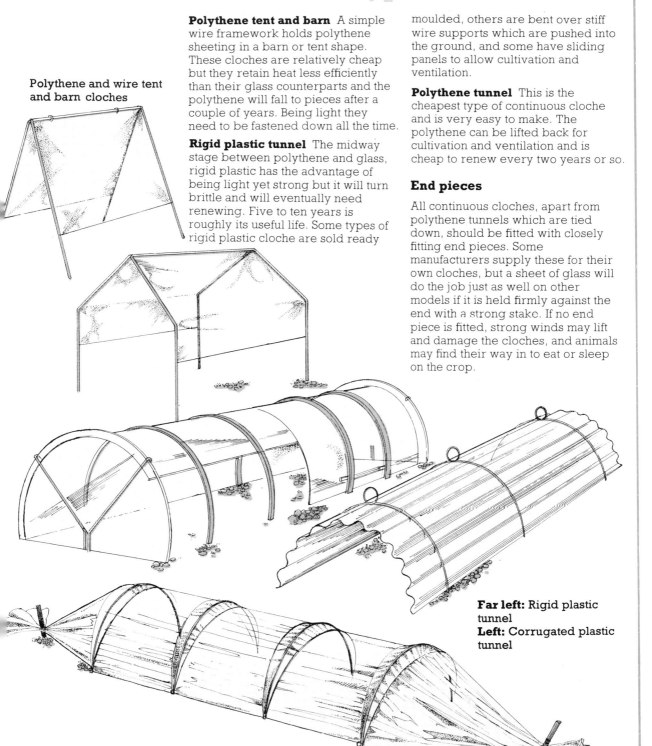

**Far left:** Rigid plastic tunnel
**Left:** Corrugated plastic tunnel

Polythene tunnel

# Cloches

As with all types of protective structure, good light is essential. Avoid placing the cloches under the canopy of trees at all costs, for the glass will become dirty as well as being shaded.

Wind is not the menace that it can be with greenhouses. Cloches are low lying and, provided that they are well anchored, should be able to stand a few powerful gusts.

If drainage is poor the soil will be slow to warm up and inhospitable to tender young roots. It will be cold, too, if it is in a frost pocket such as a hollow at the foot of a slope, or against a hedge at the lower end of your garden.

Opinions vary as to the direction cloches should run. I don't think it matters really if the light is good. If you are on a slope though, run the cloches across it rather than down it. This avoids soil erosion and also waterlogging at the lower end.

## Putting the cloches together

Back in 1912 a Major L. H. Chase developed what he called the continuous cloche. Two main designs were produced; the barn and the tent. The popularity of these cloches has never waned – the wire frames are still manufactured today and a good many old ones are to be found in potting sheds all over the country.

Faced with these strange-shaped pieces of wire you may be rather confused. If you are, shown opposite is how the Chase barn cloche is put together (the tent type you can work out yourself).

There are four pieces of wire framework needed for each cloche.

If 'A' on the base wire measures 15cm (6in), the cloche is a low barn and will need:
  2 sheets of glass 60 × 15cm
    (24 × 6in);
  2 sheets of glass 60 × 30cm
    (24 × 12in).

If 'A' on the base wire measures 30cm (12in), the cloche is a high barn and will need:
  4 sheets of glass 60 × 30cm
    (24 × 12in)

## Polythene tunnel

This type of continuous cloche you can easily make yourself. All you need is some stout but bendable wire, some strong twine and a long strip of polythene.

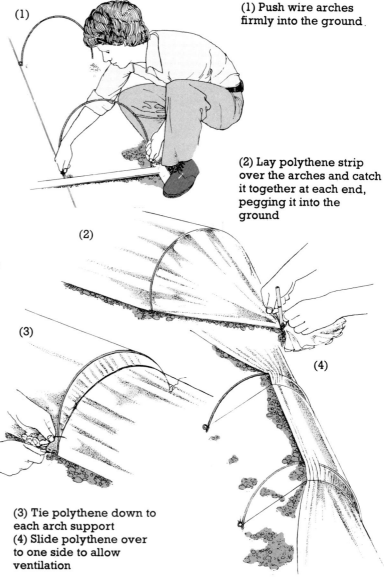

(1)

**(1) Push wire arches firmly into the ground**

**(2) Lay polythene strip over the arches and catch it together at each end, pegging it into the ground**

(2)

(3)

(4)

**(3) Tie polythene down to each arch support**
**(4) Slide polythene over to one side to allow ventilation**

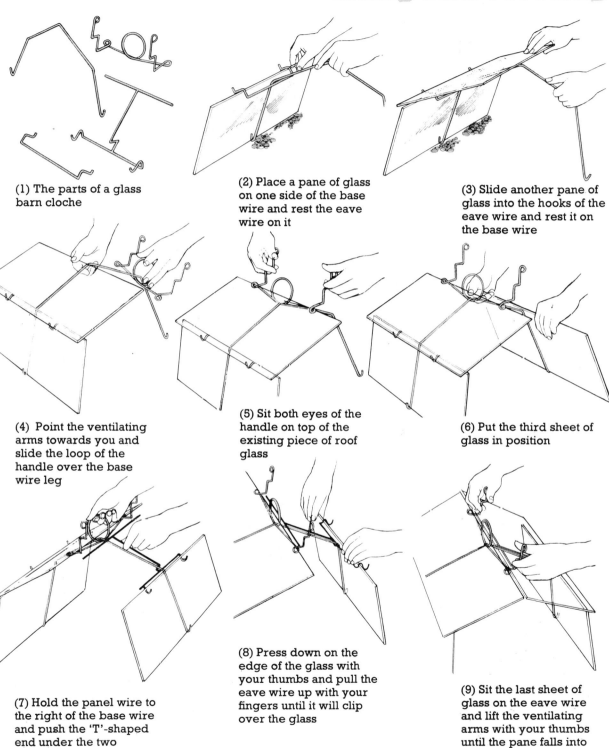

(1) The parts of a glass barn cloche

(2) Place a pane of glass on one side of the base wire and rest the eave wire on it

(3) Slide another pane of glass into the hooks of the eave wire and rest it on the base wire

(4) Point the ventilating arms towards you and slide the loop of the handle over the base wire leg

(5) Sit both eyes of the handle on top of the existing piece of roof glass

(6) Put the third sheet of glass in position

(7) Hold the panel wire to the right of the base wire and push the 'T'-shaped end under the two ventilating arms

(8) Press down on the edge of the glass with your thumbs and pull the eave wire up with your fingers until it will clip over the glass

(9) Sit the last sheet of glass on the eave wire and lift the ventilating arms with your thumbs until the pane falls into place

**61**

# Cloches

Rough, uncultivated ground should be cleared in winter of any debris and weed growth. You can use chemicals to kill off the weeds but often they can be effectively and quickly dug up, if they are thick-rooted perennials, or dug in, if they are flimsy annuals.

There are many complicated and backbreaking ways of digging but if you simply turn over the soil to one spade's depth, working backwards on short rows, you will find that on most soils the vegetables will be quite happy.

## Liming

Every soil has its own level of acidity or alkalinity which can be measured on what is known as the pH scale. It is always a good idea to test your soil with one of the simple kits available before you grow anything on it to see if it will suit a good range of plants.

If the test tells you your soil has a pH of between 6·5 and 7·0 you have no need to worry. If it is lower than 6·5 it is acid and will benefit from being limed, and if it is above 7·0 it is alkaline and acid peat or acidic fertilizers will bring it down to a more suitable level. The kit will recommend materials and quantities to be applied to a soil with a given pH value.

Wait for a month or so after digging in manure before scattering lime on the surface of the soil and leaving it to be washed in by rain.

## Fertilizers and manure

These are two of the gardener's best friends and all vegetables need them, though they vary in their preferences as to quantity. On all newly cultivated ground crops will appreciate a bucketful of well-rotted stable manure or spent mushroom compost or just plain garden compost from the heap, in each square metre (square yard) of ground. Spread this over the soil before you start to dig and work it into the top 23cm (9in).

Two or three handfuls of a general fertilizer like blood, bone and fish meal to the square metre (square yard) will again do wonders (it seems to work so much better than growmore).

## Covering up

If the cloches can be positioned on the plot as soon as it has been prepared, and left there for two or three weeks, you will find that the soil will be much easier to work at sowing or planting time.

Cloches do not heat the ground up more than a degree or two; their value lies in the fact that they prevent the surface of the soil from becoming sodden and compacted, and they provide the plant with a sheltered, well-lit atmosphere conducive to growth. Always position cloches in rows with the aid of a garden line, remove any stones which get in the way of the sides and gently bed them in to the top inch or so of soil.

## Rotation

If the same crop were to be grown year after year on the same piece of ground, pests and diseases would quickly establish themselves and the soil would become exhausted. For this reason it is wise to move crops around on the vegetable plot each year. Those which like fresh-manured ground can be given it, and those which prefer a soil which is not so rich can occupy a patch which was manured for a previous crop. Some vegetables like a light dusting of lime if the soil is slightly acid and

**To ensure your cloches are in a straight row position them against a garden line. Bed each cloche into the soil to keep it firm**

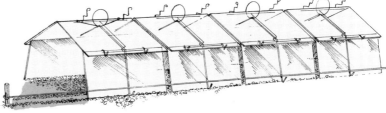

**To clear the between-row area of weeds, water on a herbicide with a dribble bar attachment on the watering can. The coarse sprinkling will not drift onto the crops at each side**

these too can be worked into a simple rotation by dividing the plot into three sections:

### Controlling Weeds

For keeping down weeds between rows of cloches there is nothing better than a Dutch hoe. Pushed through the soil regularly while the weeds are still small it will make light work of cleaning the ground. Closer to the plants hand weeding will be necessary, for if a hoe is used it can easily slip and separate root from shoot.

Crops like strawberries and beans can be kept free of weeds by mulching. This involves spreading an 8- or 10-cm (3- or 4-in) layer of well-rotted compost or manure (or even grass clippings in the case of beans) over the soil around the plants. If you lack manure or compost, black polythene can be used with strawberries – a slit being made in it for each plant to grow through. Apart from keeping down weeds, mulching also helps the soil to retain moisture and prevents mud splashing.

Wherever possible I prefer to avoid using weedkillers on cultivated ground, especially where food crops are being grown; but if you are faced with a very overgrown site to start with, and feel that you have to kill off the weeds rather than hack them down and dig them up, water them with a diluted solution of paraquat applied with a watering can fitted with a dribble bar. This coarse sprinkling prevents the spray from drifting on to cultivated plants.

Paraquat is a contact weedkiller which kills any green plants it touches. It is inactivated by the soil. Applied strictly according to the manufacturer's instructions and stored out of the reach of children and pets it is a safe product to use.

## Crop rotation plan

| | PLOT 1 | PLOT 2 | PLOT 3 |
|---|---|---|---|
| 1st YEAR | Beans<br>Celeriac<br>Celery<br>Cucumber<br>Endive<br>Leeks<br>Lettuce<br>Marrow<br>Onions<br>Peas<br>Radishes<br>Shallots<br>Spinach<br><br>1-2 bucketfuls of compost per square metre | Beetroot<br>Carrots<br>Leaf beet<br>Parsnips<br>Peppers<br>Potatoes<br>Swede<br>Sweet corn<br>Tomatoes<br>Turnips<br><br>2-3 handfuls of general fertilizer per square metre | Broccoli<br>Brussels sprouts<br>Cabbage<br>Cauliflower<br>Kale<br>Kohl rabi<br><br>light dusting of lime; 2-3 handfuls of general fertilizer per square metre |
| 2nd YEAR | PLOT 3 | PLOT 1 | PLOT 2 |
| 3rd YEAR | PLOT 2 | PLOT 3 | PLOT 1 |

# Cloches

## Watering

If you find the thought of watering a row or two of cloches rather daunting, take comfort from the fact that it will be much easier than you think and under normal weather conditions it will not be necessary very often.

Through winter and spring we are blessed in Britain with a good sprinkling of rain which seeps into the soil not only downwards but sideways as well. The largest plastic tunnel or glass cloche will be only a couple of feet wide and as both the rainwater and the plants' roots move horizontally through the soil the two will come into contact and the plant will drink. There are one or two things a gardener can do to ensure the efficiency of this system. Firstly, make sure that the soil between the cloches is well cultivated to allow water to drain through; and, secondly, keep the soil well supplied with organic matter so that the water can move quickly downwards and sideways.

In dry weather applications of water will be needed, but before rushing out with the hosepipe dig a hole in the soil with a trowel to see if it is moist underneath, for only the surface may have baked in the sun.

Seedlings and young plants with shallow root systems will be more susceptible to dryness in the top few inches of soil than mature plants and will need watering sooner. Seedlings are the only plants which will need direct watering; the cloches are removed and the ground given a gentle soaking with a watering can or hosepipe fitted with a fine rose.

Once plants are established all water is applied to the soil outside the cloches. There are several ways of doing this, apart from using a watering can or hose. An oscillating or perforated hose sprinkler can be placed among the cloches and as the water runs off the glass it will seep into the ground. On very light soils a

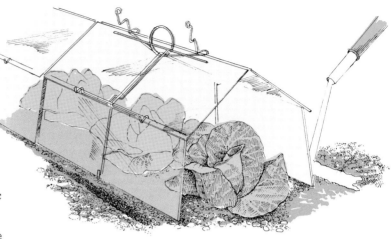

shallow channel taken out with a draw hoe down each side of a row of cloches will allow the water to collect and permeate the soil closest to the plants' roots.

If you possess any lengths of trickle irrigation tubing these too can be laid in between the rows of cloches as close to the glass as possible. A slow, steady flow of water will find its way to the plants' roots very efficiently.

Certain cloches are offered for sale which are described as being self-watering. This usually means that they have a flat roof panel which collects rain or irrigation water and allows it to drip through on to the plants and soil. Only personal

**Watering into channels on each side of the cloches will allow moisture to permeate to the plant roots**

**A self-watering cloche with its flat roof panel allows water to drip on to the soil covered by the cloche**

experience will reveal the effectiveness of this type of cloche, but its possible disadvantages are a constant gap in the glass which, although allowing ventilation, may make for premature loss of heat, and the dripping of water on to the plants being grown may set up fungal infections.

## Ventilation

Essential to provide a good flow of air which makes conditions less favourable for pests and diseases, and to reduce temperature and consequently water loss, ventilation is easily achieved on most types of cloche. Many glass cloches have wire clips which allow one of the roof

**Removing a pane of glass from a barn cloche will allow ventilation**

panes of glass to be lifted, so permitting warm air to escape. Rigid plastic types may have sliding panels which fulfil the same purpose.

More basic models which are not fitted with these sophisticated means of circulating air can be tilted upwards on one side with a brick, or spaced an inch or two further apart so that air can move between them. Polythene tunnels are easily ventilated by propping up their sides with a small piece of hardboard or timber, or even a flowerpot.

If you are ventilating on one side only, do it on the leeward so that the wind cannot suddenly whip up the cloches and break them. Remember to ventilate as often as you can – even in the middle of winter when the sun is bright or the weather is excessively humid. A once-a-day blow through will do most plants a power of good if the air is not icy cold or sopping wet.

## Shading

Seldom necessary, this is something to consider only if the cloches are being used over crops like tomatoes, melons and cucumbers in late spring and summer, or when the sun is bright and young seedlings are being scorched. One of the proprietary whitewash compounds will be effective if applied to the glass in a thin coating, but remember to check its suitability if your cloches are made of plastic and to wash it off before using them again in winter and spring.

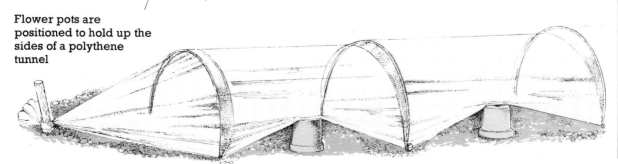

**Flower pots are positioned to hold up the sides of a polythene tunnel**

# Cloche cropping programme

Cloches can be used to hasten the development of many vegetables, but the ones really worth covering are those which can be encouraged to mature while their shop prices are high or when they would be otherwise unobtainable. Fruit is worth forcing too. Strawberries and melons are especially well-suited to being cloche grown.

## Broad bean

*Varieties:* Aquadulce, The Sutton.
*Sow:* November, 5cm (2in) deep, 15cm (6in) apart in double rows 23cm (9in) apart.
*Cloches on ground:* Two weeks before sowing (use high barn type).
*Cloches off:* Early March.
*Harvest:* May-June onwards. Try picking young pods and preparing as for French or runner beans.

## Courgette or marrow

*Varieties:* Zucchini, Golden Zucchini.
*Sow:* Early May. Three seeds in one spot every 1m (3ft) along row. Thin to leave strongest seedling.
*Cloches on ground:* Two weeks before sowing.
*Cloches off:* Early June.
*Harvest:* July onwards.

## French bean

*Varieties:* The Prince, Masterpiece.
*Sow:* Late April, 2·5cm (1in) deep and 8cm (3in) apart.
*Cloches on ground:* Two weeks before sowing (high barn type).
*Cloches off:* Early June.
*Harvest:* July onwards.

## Lettuce

*Varieties:* Imperial Winter, Fortune, Kwiek.
*Sow:* September-October (Imperial Winter), late January (Fortune), late August (Kwiek). Thinly in 0·5cm ($\frac{1}{4}$in) deep drills 20cm (8in) apart. Thin to 23cm (9in). Barn cloche should take three rows.
*Cloches on:* Two weeks before sowing (Imperial Winter and Fortune), October-November (Kwiek).
*Cloches off:* April (Imperial Winter), May (Fortune), after picking (Kwiek).
*Harvest:* March-May (Imperial Winter), May-June (Fortune), November-December (Kwiek).

## Melon

*Varieties:* Charantais, Sweetheart.
*Plant out:* Early June.
*Cloches on ground:* At planting time (high or low barn type).
*Cloches off:* July, or can be left on in northern areas to give protection until cropping finished.
*Harvest:* August-September.

## Peas

*Varieties:* Meteor, Feltham First.
*Sow:* October (Meteor), late February (Feltham First), in flat-bottomed drills 4cm (1$\frac{1}{2}$in) deep and 23cm (9in) wide.
*Cloches on ground:* Two weeks before sowing (high barn type).
*Cloches off:* Early April (Meteor), mid-April (Feltham First).
*Harvest:* Late May-June (Meteor), June-July (Feltham First).

## Potatoes

*Varieties:* Red Duke Of York, Harbinger.
*Plant:* Late February, 13cm (5in) deep and 30cm (12in) apart in single rows.
*Cloches on ground:* Two weeks before planting (high barn type).
*Cloches off:* When harvested.
*Harvest:* Mid-May to June.

## Radish

*Varieties:* French Breakfast, Red Forcing.
*Sow:* September-October and February. Thinly 1cm ($\frac{1}{2}$in) deep in rows 15cm (6in) apart.
*Cloches on ground:* After sowing (September-October), two weeks before sowing (February).
*Cloches off:* When harvested.
*Harvest:* As soon as large enough to eat. Will mature quickly (8-10 weeks) so can be sown as a catch-crop between slower-growing vegetables and pulled before the space is needed.

## Runner beans

*Varieties:* Enorma, Mergoles.
*Sow:* Mid-April. Two seeds at each station 5cm (2in) deep and 30cm (1ft) apart in a double row 45cm (18in) apart.
*Cloches on ground:* Two weeks before sowing.
*Cloches off:* Late May-early June. Stake as soon as cloches removed.
*Harvest:* Mid- to late July onwards.

## Strawberries

*Varieties:* Pantagruella, Tamella.
*Plant:* Late July-August, 30cm (12in) apart in a double row 25cm (10in) apart.
*Cloches on ground:* February. Remove all runners.
*Cloches off:* After harvesting.
*Harvest:* Late May onwards. (Force for one year only.)

## Sweet corn

*Varieties:* John Innes Hybrid, First of All.
*Sow:* Late April. Two seeds 5cm (2in) deep at each 25cm (10in) station along the row. With wide cloches sow double rows 38cm (15in) apart. Remove weakest seedling at each station.
*Cloches on ground:* Two weeks before sowing.
*Cloches off:* When leaves touch ridge.
*Harvest:* Late July onwards.

## Sweet peppers (Capsicum)

*Varieties:* Canape, Worldbeater.
*Plant out:* Late May, 45cm (18in) apart in single rows.
*Cloches on ground:* At planting time (high barn type).
*Cloches off:* Late June, or after harvesting in northern areas.
*Harvest:* August onwards.

## Tomatoes

*Varieties:* The Amateur, Pixie (both bush types).
*Plant out:* Mid-April. Single rows, plants 60cm (2ft) apart.
*Cloches on ground:* Two weeks before planting (high barn type).
*Cloches off:* Early to mid-June. Stand cloches on bricks if plants reach ridge before this.
*Harvest:* Late July onwards.

## Turnips

*Varieties:* Jersey Navet, Snowball.
*Sow:* Late February. Thinly, 1cm ($\frac{1}{2}$in) deep in rows 30cm (1ft) apart. Thin seedlings to 15cm (6in).
*Cloches on ground:* Two weeks before sowing.
*Cloches off:* Mid-April.
*Harvest:* June onwards when roots size of a tennis ball.

## Cloche cropping programme

The few minutes spent working out a programme for your cloches will make sure that they are utilized to their full extent. The suggestions below will help to keep them occupied all the year round. Like those in the frame programme (see page 57), any crops which need covering at the same time, e.g. French and runner beans, can be interchanged.

| | Jan | Feb | Mar | Apr | May | Jun | Jul | Aug | Sep | Oct | Nov | Dec |
|---|---|---|---|---|---|---|---|---|---|---|---|---|
| **1** | | | | Sweet corn | | | | | | | | |
| | | | | | | Melons | | | | | | |
| | Broad beans (cont) | | | | | | | | | | Broad beans | |
| **2** | Radishes | | | | | | | | | | | |
| | | | | | French beans | | | | | | | |
| | | | | | | Sweet peppers | | | | | | |
| | Peas: Meteor (cont) | | | | | | | | Peas: Meteor | | | |
| **3** | | | Turnips | | | | | | | | | |
| | | | | | Runner beans | | | | | | | |
| | | | | | | Melons | | | | | | |
| | Lettuce: Imperial Winter (cont) | | | | | | | | | Lettuce: Imperial Winter | | |
| **4** | | | Strawberries | | | | | | | | | |
| | | | | | | Sweet peppers | | | | | | |
| | | | | | | | | | Radishes | | | |
| **5** | Peas: Feltham First | | | | | | | | | | | |
| | | | | | Tomatoes | | | | | | | |
| | | | | | | Melons | | | | | | |
| | | | | | | | | | Lettuce: Kwiek | | | |

# Cloches

Cloches don't have to be confined to the vegetable plot. In flower borders and rock gardens they can be put to good use in protecting plants susceptible to winter wet.

Many rock plants spend the winter in their natural surroundings covered in snow which, rather surprisingly, keeps them dry. Only when spring comes and the snow melts do they get the good drink necessary to start them on their way. The wet winters of non-alpine climates often cause these plants to rot off, but a single cloche (without ends) will keep out the wet while allowing good ventilation. When placed over clumps of Christmas roses (*Helleborus niger*) the cloches will not only encourage the flowers to develop more quickly, but they will also protect the white blooms from mud splashing.

## Raising seedlings

A small patch of good soil in a sunny corner of the garden can be treated as a nursery for cabbages, cauliflowers, broccoli, Brussels sprouts, leeks and onions which can be transplanted to the vegetable plot when they are of a fair size and the ground is ready for them.

Half-hardy annuals and bedding plants need not be out of reach for the gardener without a greenhouse. Under a short row of cloches many of them can be raised in April and May, thinned out and later transplanted to their flowering quarters in beds, borders, hanging baskets, window boxes and pots.

## Sheltering

In exposed gardens where protection is needed more against wind than cold, cloches may be used in a different fashion. Newly planted tomatoes or peppers can be surrounded by a couple of the tent or barn type stood on end. Where winds are continuous this form of protection may be left in place all summer. To prevent the cloches

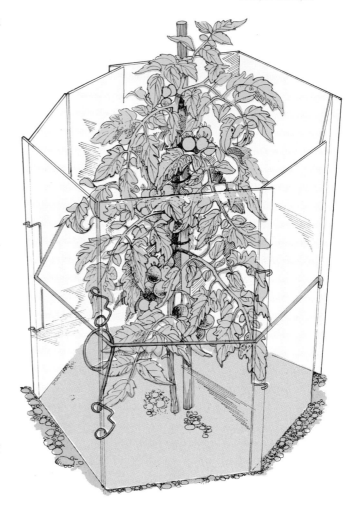

**A tomato plant protected by two barn cloches stood on end**

themselves from being blown over tie a length of strong twine around them, looping it through their handles. Alternatively, push a cane through each handle and in to the soil.

## Ripening

If you lack a dry shed in which to ripen off onions and shallots at the end of their growing season, look to your cloches. Spaced so that a little air flows between the gaps, a row can be positioned over the lifted bulbs which are laid on the surface of the soil. When the tops of the bulbs have dried off the cloches can be removed and the bulbs cleaned and stored.

In less than tropical summers outdoor tomatoes frequently fail to ripen all their fruits. When this happens the plants can be cut from their canes, laid on a bed of straw or a thin layer of dry peat, and covered with cloches. Here they will redden up quite quickly and when the weather turns cold any remaining fruits can be cut and ripened indoors.

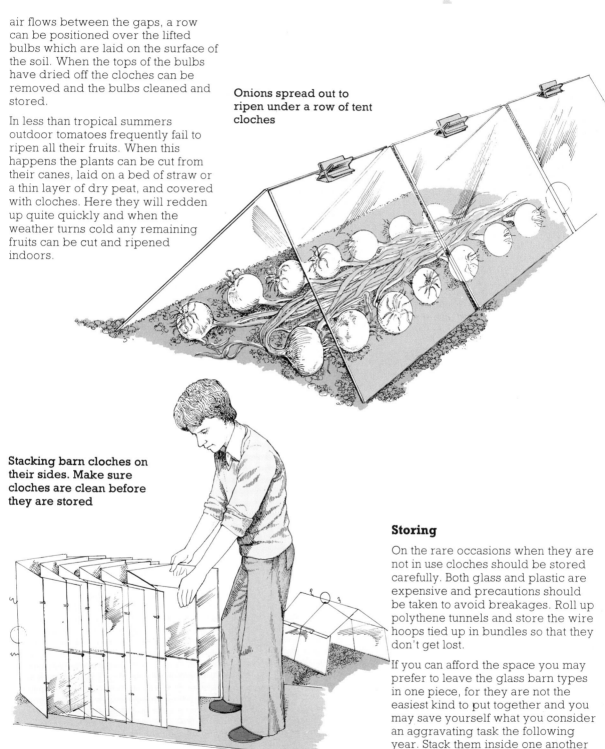

Onions spread out to ripen under a row of tent cloches

Stacking barn cloches on their sides. Make sure cloches are clean before they are stored

## Storing

On the rare occasions when they are not in use cloches should be stored carefully. Both glass and plastic are expensive and precautions should be taken to avoid breakages. Roll up polythene tunnels and store the wire hoops tied up in bundles so that they don't get lost.

If you can afford the space you may prefer to leave the glass barn types in one piece, for they are not the easiest kind to put together and you may save yourself what you consider an aggravating task the following year. Stack them inside one another standing them on their ends.

# Controlling pests and diseases

Even if you are the world's most fastidious gardener and your crops the healthiest around, sooner or later you are bound to be faced with a pest or disease outbreak. The important thing to do is to make sure that your crops will at least have the stamina to resist these attacks.

Firstly, always grow plants propagated from healthy stock and keep them vigorous and in peak condition by providing them with sufficient food and ideal growing conditions.

Be hygienic – don't leave weeds or old plant pots lying around, for they can harbour infection, and always use sterile potting and seed composts. Wash down greenhouses, cloches and frames at some point each year to destroy lurking pests and fungal spores. When you do discover an outbreak of a particular pest or disease, act quickly – it may save you a lot of work a few days later.

## Pest, disease or disorder?

Various organisms can infect plants to the detriment of their health.

**Pests** The majority of these are insects, but problems are also encountered with mites (e.g. red spider mite) and molluscs (slugs and snails). Different chemicals are needed to control each of these types of pest. Insects are killed with insecticides, mites with acaricides and slugs and snails with molluscicides – usually more descriptively known as slug baits or pellets.

**Diseases** Three distinct types of organisms are responsible here: fungi, bacteria and viruses. The first two can usually be controlled by chemical and cultural means but the viruses are usually incurable and the plants must be destroyed. Unchecked viruses will cause degeneration and a reduction in vigour and yield.

**Disorders** These are not the result of a disease infection, although the symptoms shown are often attributed to disease. Physiological disorders, to give them their full title, occur as a result of faults in cultivation or when plants are grown in an unsuitable environment. Plants suffering from disorders can often be brought back into good health by adjustment of growing conditions.

## The remedies

The range of products available to gardeners for putting paid to pest and disease problems is phenomenal. It is easy to be tempted to rush into the garden brandishing a sprayer at the first sign of a plump greenfly, but try to be a little more practical.

Small outbreaks of both pests and diseases can often be controlled by simply picking off and destroying. Caterpillars or infected leaves can be pulled off individually, and minor colonies of greenfly squashed between the fingers. This may not be a pleasant experience but it does work.

When you have to reach for a chemical make sure you know what it does and what the alternatives are:

**Sprays** These are liquids or powders diluted in water and squirted in mist form on to the plant through a pressurized jet. Many hand-pumped plastic sprayers are available. Pick one which is of a comfortable design and does not leak, and wash it out thoroughly after use.

**Aerosols** Pressurized canisters containing various chemicals which are ready for immediate application. Always hold the aerosol at least 30cm (1ft) away from the plant when spraying and dispose of it in the dustbin (without puncturing) after use.

**Fumigants** Just like fireworks to look at, these smoke bombs are for use in greenhouses. The poisonous

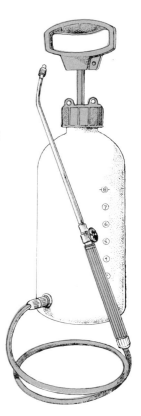

Two kinds of sprayers.
**Above:** A hand spray for small infestations
**Below:** A pump sprayer for spraying large areas

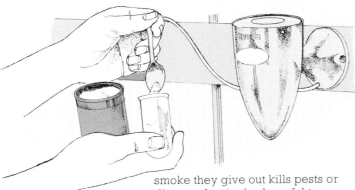

Fumigate in the evening, making sure all vents and doors are closed.
**Above:** An electric fumigator
**Below:** A smoke bomb

Cover slug bait with a piece of slate so as not to endanger pets or children

smoke they give out kills pests or diseases but is also harmful to children and pets, so check that the greenhouse is empty before, and locked during, fumigation. Make it as airtight as possible. Nicotine shreds look like shredded cardboard and are lit and stamped out so that they smoulder and give off poisonous smoke. Always fumigate in the evening when the sun has gone down, and do not enter the greenhouse till the following morning.

Electric fumigators are also available. These vapourize small amounts of insecticide or fungicide very slowly and work both day and night. Personally I don't like the idea of chemicals hovering in the greenhouse atmosphere all the time, even if they are supposed to be harmless to man.

**Dusts** These are fine powders which are usually applied to infected plants through plastic 'puffer packs'. Try to coat the plants with a thin film of dust rather than dense, uneven patches. Insecticidal dusts can be worked into the soil to control subterranean pests. They are usually scattered from a large pepper-pot type of dispenser.

**Baits** Slugs, snails and also cockroaches are killed with poisoned baits laid on their trails. Cover small piles of bait with pieces of slate or tile or scatter pellets deep among the foliage of plants to protect animals and children. Heavy rain will break down slug pellets and they should be replaced at intervals.

## Safety

To cut risks to a minimum always observe the following safety precautions when using garden chemicals:

**1** READ THE MANUFACTURER'S INSTRUCTIONS AND FOLLOW THEM CAREFULLY.

**2** Take the added precaution of wearing a pair of rubber gloves when handling any chemical and wash your hands and face afterwards.

**3** Never make the solution more concentrated than the manufacturer recommends – it will damage the plants rather than the pest or disease.

**4** Observe the time lapses specified by the manufacturer to be allowed between spraying and harvesting.

**5** Insecticides applied to control harmful insects will also kill beneficial ones. Bees are especially susceptible so always spray in the evening when most of them are safely back in the hive.

**6** Avoid mixing more solution than you will need, but dispose of any surplus by flushing it down the lavatory. Empty chemical containers should be capped tightly and put in the dustbin.

**7** STORE ALL CHEMICALS IN CLEARLY LABELLED CONTAINERS WELL OUT OF THE REACH OF CHILDREN AND ANIMALS.

## Trade names

The chemicals mentioned on the following charts are offered for sale under various trade names. The manufacturers listed on p.77 will recommend suitable products from their own ranges, or you can consult a very useful booklet entitled Directory of Garden Chemicals, which is available from the British Agrochemicals Association, Alembic House, 93, Albert Embankment, London SE 1.

# Pests under cover

| Pest | Description and Damage Caused | Plants Attacked | Means of Control |
|---|---|---|---|
| **Ants** | Small, fast-moving insects, too well known to need description. 'Farm' greenfly for honeydew and disturb soil in borders, boxes and pots. | A wide range of plants is affected by their activities. | Various ant-destroying powders are offered which vary in their effectiveness. 'Nippon', sold as a jelly, seems to be particularly good. Where nest is accessible, drench with boiling water. |
| **Carrot fly** | Small white larvae eat into roots. Foliage develops a reddish tinge and wilts. | Carrots (occasionally parsnips). | Dust around young plants with bromophos. A paraffin-soaked rag dragged over the foliage once a month from April to June is also supposed to be a good deterrent. |
| **Caterpillars** | Large, long grubs of various colours. Foliage is systematically eaten away. Black droppings can be seen on leaves. | A wide range, especially seedling brassicas. | Where damage is confined to one plant, pick off caterpillars by hand and destroy. Where widespread, spray plants with derris or malathion. |
| **Celery fly** | Small white grubs tunnel into foliage leaving hollow creamy areas which look like blisters. Plants' vigour suffers. | Celery, celeriac, often while still in boxes before being planted out. | Pick off leaves and destroy if only one or two affected. In severe attacks spray fortnightly with malathion. |
| **Cutworms** | Large, fat, greyish-cream caterpillars which curl up when disturbed. Found in soil. Eat plant roots and stem bases. Plants wilt or lose vigour. | A wide range of plants attacked in soil of garden, frame or greenhouse. | Insecticide such as bromophos should be forked into soil during cultivation. Pick out and destroy grubs found at any time. |
| **Earwigs** | Long brown insects with pincer-like 'tails'. Flowers and foliage eaten away. | A small range of crops are attacked. | Earwigs can be trapped in plant pots filled with straw and inverted on canes stuck in the soil. Empty pots into boiling water daily. |
| **Eelworms** | Minute worm-like insects; most cannot be seen with the naked eye. Leaves may become distorted (narcissus) or browned (chrysanthemum) and roots knotted (tomato). All plants lose vigour. | Tomatoes, chrysanthemums, narcissi, phlox, onions, potatoes. | Control is difficult. Dig up and burn infected plants and do not replant with same crop for several years. Control weeds which may acts as hosts. Practise crop rotation. |
| **Flea beetle** | Seedlings have punctured and spotted leaves as a result of being eaten by this tiny black beetle. | Seedlings of many crops, especially brassicas, turnips and radishes. | Well-nourished plants can withstand attack better than starved ones. Dust seedlings with derris shortly after they emerge. |
| **Greenfly** | Small, fat-bodied green flies (or black flies) known correctly as aphids. Suck sap, weakening plants and transmit virus diseases. Secrete messy honeydew. | Almost any plant can be attacked by this widespread pest. | Rub off minor infestations with fingers. Spray with dimethoate or malathion. Fumigate greenhouses with HCH canisters or nicotine shreds. |
| **Leaf miner** | Small creamy-coloured grubs tunnel into leaves, disfiguring them. | Chrysanthemums, cinerarias. | In isolated instances remove and destroy infested leaves. In more serious infestations, spray with malathion. |
| **Leatherjackets** | Long grey legless caterpillars found in soil. Larvae of daddy longlegs. Roots eaten. Plants may wilt and lose vigour in consequence. | A wide range of crops grown in soil in greenhouse, frame or garden. | Fork insecticidal dust such as carbaryl into soil when cultivating ground. |

| Pest | Description and Damage Caused | Plants Attacked | Means of Control |
|------|------------------------------|-----------------|------------------|
| **Mealy bug** | Small, white bugs covered in waxy wool deposit. Usually found in leaf axils where they suck sap and secrete honeydew. | Wide range of greenhouse plants – mainly ornamentals, especially ferns and palms, but also grape vines. | Spray with derris or pyrethrum. Fumigate greenhouse with nicotine shreds. Remove stubborn colonies with cotton wool soaked in liquid derris. |
| **Narcissus fly** | Large creamy-white grubs feed inside bulbs causing them to rot rather than grow. | Narcissus (including daffodils), hyacinths, snowdrops and bluebells. | Destroy all infested bulbs. Purchase bulbs from a reputable source to be sure that they are free of the pest. |
| **Pea and bean weevil** | Small brown beetle-like insects which chew the edge of pea and bean foliage giving it a scalloped appearance. | Peas and broad beans in seedling and mature stages. | Even fairly severe attacks of this pest are unlikely to do any real harm. Spray with derris if the damage becomes serious. |
| **Red spider mite** | Foliage becomes bleached and small pinhead-sized mites, brown or cream colour, can be seen on the underside of leaves. Fine webbing is produced. | Many greenhouse plants. Strawberries indoors and out. | Keep atmosphere moist to discourage attack. Spray with malathion or dimethoate. Fumigate greenhouse with nicotine. |
| **Scale insects** | Small brown scales, like legless tortoises, found on stems and leaves. Reduce vigour of plants by sucking sap. Secretes honeydew. | Many greenhouse plants, especially vines and glossy-leaved ornamentals. | Spray with malathion. Fumigate greenhouse with nicotine. |
| **Slugs and snails** | Too well known to need description. Foliage and stems eaten as well as roots. Silvery trail often left behind. | Wide range of seedlings and mature plants. | Lay poisoned baits (pellets are best) out of the reach of animals and children (under a piece of slate or in a short length of drainpipe). |
| **Strawberry eelworm** | Minute pest which causes crown of plant to die out and leaves to become distorted. Usually seen in May. | Strawberries in open ground. | Destroy infected plants. Buy in new stock and grow on new ground. Practise crop rotation. |
| **Symphilids** | Like white centipedes, these insects may eat the young roots of plants in greenhouse borders. Outbreaks of this pest are not very common. | Cucumbers and tomatoes. | Fork HCH into soil during cultivations. |
| **Tarsonemid mite** | Small mites (not unlike red spider mite) attack plants on undersides of leaves. Foliage turns purple, becomes brittle and falls, flowers wither and become distorted. | Strawberries, begonias, cyclamen, fuchsias, saintpaulias and geraniums (pelargoniums). | Dust with flowers of sulphur. |
| **Thrips** | Small dark-brown insects which suck sap from leaves and flowers causing them to become distorted and streaked. | Wide range of plants including carnations and chrysanthemums. | Ventilate greenhouse to keep temperature cool, and spray plants with water to discourage attack. Spray with malathion. Fumigate greenhouse with nicotine. |
| **Vine weevil** | Creamy-white grubs feed on roots and storage organs, often causing the attacked plant to keel over. | Cyclamen and begonia corms, and ferns. | Discard infested plants and soil. Use sterilized compost and buy healthy plants or corms. |
| **Whitefly** | Small white flies which fly rapidly in circles when disturbed. Colonize undersides of plants' leaves sucking sap. Immature stages appear as white scales. | Many greenhouse plants. | Spray with malathion at fortnightly intervals to kill emerging flies. |

# Diseases and disorders under cover

| Disease or Disorder | Symptoms | Plants Attacked | Means of Control |
|---|---|---|---|
| **Blackleg** | Stems rot and turn black just above soil level. Plants die as a result. Caused by grey mould (see below). | Tomatoes, cucumbers, melons, pelargoniums and other ornamentals. | Keep greenhouse well ventilated. Usually occurs in cold, damp greenhouses especially in winter when air is stagnant. Fumigate with tecnazene; spray with captan. Remove and destroy infected plants. Keep greenhouse clean. |
| **Blossom end rot** | Fruits develop black, rather sunken areas at the end furthest from the stalk. | Tomatoes. | This disorder occurs when the soil has been allowed to dry out, though it may not appear for a week or so. Water carefully, keeping the soil gently moist. |
| **Blotchy ripening** | Fruits colour up unevenly with red, green and yellow blotches. | Tomatoes. | Ensure adequate potash in soil. Dress borders with sulphate of potash at the rate of 30 g to the square metre (1 oz to the square yard) if the disorder has previously been in evidence. |
| **Chlorosis** | Foliage yellow and rather stunted. | A wide range of plants. | Disorder is due to shortage of magnesium or iron. Usually encountered on chalky soils. Water plants with sequestrene. Check that soil is well manured and fertilized. |
| **Chocolate spot** | Leaves develop small brown spots and stems brown streaks. Leaves may turn completely brown and wilt in severe attacks. | Broad beans – especially if autumn sown. | Give the plants a well-manured, well-fertilized piece of ground which is sheltered. They should then grow away healthily. Spray badly infected plants with Bordeaux mixture. |
| **Damping off** | Seedlings keel over and die due to base of stem rotting. | A very wide range of seedlings. | Prevalent in a warm, humid atmosphere. Ventilate carefully, allowing in fresh air but still maintaining a reasonable temperature. Sow thinly. Water seedlings with Cheshunt compound. |
| **Galls** | Crinkly outgrowths usually at the base of the plant's stem. | Pelargoniums. | These galls do no great harm. Break them off and destroy them. Do not propagate from infected plants or the galls will persist. |
| **Greenback** | A similar disorder to blotchy ripening (see above). The end of the fruit nearest the stalk stays green, refusing to ripen. | Tomatoes. | Ensure adequate potash in soil (see Blotchy ripening). Protect plants from excessively strong sunshine. Certain varieties are resistant to this disorder – choose them if it is a problem. |
| **Grey mould** | Stems and leaves rot off and are covered in a grey, fluffy outgrowth (correctly known as botrytis). | Many plants and cuttings in the process of being rooted. | Ensure good ventilation but a fairly warm atmosphere. Avoid keeping foliage wet. Keep greenhouse clean. Spray with captan; fumigate greenhouse with tecnazene. |
| **Mildew** | A powdery white fungal outgrowth which may eventually turn brown and cause plant tissue to rot. Reduces plants' vigour. | Wide range including chrysanthemums, vines, lettuces, cinerarias and stocks. | Ensure good ventilation but a fairly warm atmosphere. Spray with benomyl. |

| Disease or Disorder | Symptoms | Plants Attacked | Means of Control |
|---|---|---|---|
| **Potato blight** | Fruits develop dark brown areas and eventually rot completely. | Tomatoes. | Spray with zineb in early July if the disease has previously been a problem. Dig up and destroy all infected plants. |
| **Red core** | Plants wilt. If dug up, roots will be stringy and mouse-tail like. If cut open they will reveal a central red stripe. | Strawberries. | Dig up and destroy infected plants. Grow resistant varieties. Improve soil drainage – this disease usually occurs on waterlogged ground. |
| **Root rot** | Plants wilt starting at the shoot tips, and as the trouble becomes more acute the wilting spreads downwards. | Tomatoes. | Water carefully – allowing plants to become neither too wet nor too dry. Keep temperature sufficiently high. Topdress infected plants with peaty compost, shade from hot sun and spray with water. |
| **Rust** | Several diseases, most of which produce orange or brown powdery spots on leaves. | Chrysanthemums, carnations, antirrhinums and other plants. | Remove and destroy badly infected leaves. Spray with thiram or zineb at fortnightly intervals. |
| **Scalding** | Edges of leaves turn light brown and wither and light-brown patches appear. Fruits turn brown and shrivel, possibly only on one side. | Grapes and many young plants. | Usually caused by scorching sun. Shade plants and spray occasionally with water. May be caused by paraffin fumes, in which case scalding will not be on one side only. |
| **Sooty mould** | A black, downy outgrowth on leaves and stems which cuts out light and so reduces vigour. | A wide range of ornamental plants. | Control greenfly, whitefly and scale insects. The mould grows on the honeydew these three secrete. A sponge dipped in water will remove sooty moulds easily. |
| **Stem rot** | Stem rots just above ground level and plant collapses. | Tomatoes, cucumbers and melons. | Plant melon and cucumber slightly high on mounds of compost. Avoid splashing water around and keep temperatures sufficiently high. |
| **Strawberry leaf spot** | Leaves are covered in small red spots and may wither. Not a serious disease. | Strawberries. | Burn off foliage with straw after cropping. |
| **Tomato leaf mould** | Leaves develop yellow spots. These enlarge until the leaves wither and develop a rusty-coloured mould. | Tomatoes. | Ventilate well to avoid a humid atmosphere. Spray with thiram. Grow resistant varieties. |
| **Tulip fire** | Leaves and flowers develop strawy-coloured streaks. Flowers often fail to open. | Tulips. | Spray with thiram if disease has previously been a problem. Grow tulips on different ground each year. Destroy infected plants. |
| **Viruses** | Yellow mottling, mosaic, distortion and crinkling of foliage. Plants disfigured and weakened. | A very wide range of plants. | Dig up and burn infected plants. Never propagate from virus-infected stock. |
| **Wilt** | Plants wilt (usually from the bottom upwards), though they may recover temporarily only to wilt again until they eventually collapse. Known as 'sleepy disease' or verticillium. | Tomatoes. | Grow in healthy soil. Keep plants warm and shaded from bright sunshine. Spray foliage daily with water. Drench soil with Cheshunt compound. Destroy infected plants. |

# List of suppliers

## Greenhouses

Alitex Ltd., Station Road, Alton, Hants. (Aluminium)

Alton Greenhouses, PO Box 3, Bewdley, Worcs. (Aluminium and cedar)

Baco Leisure Products Ltd., Glebe Road, Huntingdon, Cambs. (Aluminium)

Banbury Greenhouses, PO Box 35, Kidderminster, Worcs. (Aluminium and cedar)

Cases Ltd., Taffs Well, Cardiff. (Aluminium and cedar)

Crittall Warmlife Ltd., Crittall Road, Witham, Essex. (Aluminium)

Edenlite Ltd., Hawksworth, Swindon, Wilts. (Aluminium)

Florada Garden Products, Dollar Street, Cirencester, Gloucs. (Aluminium, curved eaves)

Garden Relax, 113 Wennington Road, Rainham, Essex. (Polythene)

Lawrence Gray Ltd., Station Road, Little Chalfont, Bucks. (Timber and rigid plastic, uneven span)

Growth Cell Products, 11 Monmouth View, Llanbradach, Glamorgan. (Polythene dome)

Halls Homes and Gardens Ltd., Church Road, Paddock Wood, Kent. (Aluminium and cedar)

Kenkast Buildings Ltd., Astley, Manchester. (Aluminium and cedar)

Marley Greenhouses Ltd., Storrington, Sussex. (Aluminium, including octagonal and mini-lean-to)

Park Lines & Co., 501 Green Lanes, London N13. (Cedar, including shed and greenhouse combined)

F. Pratten & Co., Midsomer Norton, Bath. (Aluminium and cedar)

Q Cloche Ltd., Willowbank Wharf, Ranelagh Gardens, Putney Bridge, London SW6. (Mini-free-standing)

Solardome, Rosedale Engineers Ltd. Hunmanby, Filey, Yorks. (Aluminium and glass dome)

Transatlantic Plastics Ltd., Garden Estate, Ventnor, Isle of Wight. (Polythene)

Tropical Greenhouses, 14 Sanderson Street, Sheffield. (Aluminium, including octagonal)

C. H. Whitehouse Ltd., Buckhurst Works, Frant, Sussex. (Aluminium and cedar, including hexagonal)

## Garden frames

Available from many manufacturers and also:

Access Frames, Yelverton Road, Crick, Northampton

Europa Manor Engineers Ltd., Oxford Road, Brackley, Northants

Expandite Ltd., Western Road, Bracknell, Berkshire

J. T. Lowe (Longham) Ltd., Hame Lane, Longham, Wimborne, Dorset

Safe Grow Garden Products, Borden (UK) Ltd., Colley Lane Trading Estate, Bridgwater, Somerset

Simplex of Cambridge Ltd., Sawston, Cambridge

## Cloches

Agriframes Ltd., Charlwoods Road, East Grinstead, Sussex. (Polythene)

Auriol (Guildford) Ltd., Passfield, Liphook, Hants. (Semi-rigid plastic)

Essex Garden Products Ltd., Well Lane, Danbury, Essex. (Rigid plastic, sliding top)

Expandite Ltd., Western Road, Bracknell, Berks. (Chase barn and tent type wire frames)

Hyware Cloches, North West Plastics Ltd., Worsley, Manchester. (Rigid plastic)

Safe Grow Garden Products, Borden (UK) Ltd., Colley Lane Trading Estate, Bridgwater, Somerset. (Rigid plastic)

Transatlantic Plastics Ltd., Garden Estate, Ventnor, Isle of Wight. (Polythene)

Westray Cloches, 15 Church Road, Upper Boddington, Daventry, Northants. (Barn and tent types fitted with netting)

## Cloche clips

Johnson Aldridge Ltd., Longbridge Trading Estate, Mobberley Road, Knutsford, Cheshire

Rumsey Clips, 20 Beacon Down Avenue, Plymouth, Devon

# Equipment

The full address of each firm is given the first time it is mentioned.

## Timber preservatives

Cuprinol Ltd., Adderwell House, Frome, Somerset. (Cedar and other wood preservatives based on copper naphthenate)

## Anti-condensation spray for polythene houses

Clovis Lande Associates Ltd., Gaza Trading Estate, Weald, Hildenborough, Kent. (Sun Clear)

## Heaters

Aladdin Industries Ltd., Housewares Division, Brenda Road, Hartlepool, Cleveland, (Paraffin)

George H. Elt Ltd., Eltex Works, Worcester. (Paraffin)

Humex Ltd., 5 High Road, Byfleet, Weybridge, Surrey. (Electric)

The Metallic Constructions Co. (Derby) Ltd., Bridge Works, Alfreton Road, Derby. (Solid fuel and oil fired)

Shilton Garden Products, 390 City Road, London EC1. (Natural gas)

## Electrical equipment

Humex Ltd.

Jemp Engineering Ltd., Canal Estate, Station Road, Longley, Bucks

Simplex of Cambridge Ltd., Sawston, Cambridge

## Insulation material

(Polythene bubble type)

Edenlite Ltd., Hawksworth, Swindon, Wilts. (Tri-glaze)

A. Latter & Co., 43 South End, Croydon, Surrey. (Thermashield)

## Automatic ventilators

Bayliss Autovents Ltd., Compton Street, Ashbourne, Derbyshire. (Bayliss Autovent)

Humex Ltd. (Ventmaster)

Jemp Engineering Ltd. (Jempvent)

Simplex of Cambridge. (Thermofor)

## Shading compounds

Clovis Lande Associates Ltd. (Varishade)

Pan Britannica Industries, Britannica House, Waltham Cross, Herts. (Coolglass)

## Blinds

Joseph Bentley Ltd., Barrow-on-Humber, South Humberside. (Various including muslin)

Humex Ltd.

Jemp Engineering Ltd.

Netlon Ltd., Mill Hill, Blackburn, Lancs. (Netting type)

Simplex of Cambridge

## Thermometers

Joseph Bentley Ltd.

## Gravel trays

Stewart Plastics Ltd., Purley Way, Croydon, Surrey

## Water butts

Harcostar Ltd., Windover Road, Huntingdon

## Watering cans

Geeco Works, Gore Road Industrial Estate, New Milton, Hants

Harcostar Ltd.

Haws Elliott Ltd., Walsall, Staffs

## Hosepipes and hose accessories

Hozelock Ltd., Haddenham, Aylesbury, Bucks

Nethergreen Products, PO Box 13, Alderley Edge, Cheshire

Poly-gard Products, Halesowen Industrial Park, Halesowen, West Midlands

## Capillary watering systems

ICI, Plant Protection, Fernhurst, Haslemere, Surrey

Nethergreen Products

## Spaghetti-tube watering system

Nethergreen Products

## Perforated hoses

The Magni Reflector Co. Ltd., 10 Market Road, Chichester, Sussex. (Supplex hose)

## Overhead spraylines

Nethergreen Products

## Plant pots and trays

Bill and Ben, 60 Station Road, Sawbridgeworth, Bishop's Stortford, Herts. (Clay pots)
The Fyba Pot Co., Malvern Road, Knottingley, West Yorkshire. (Whalehide pots and tomato rings; cardboard pots)
Jiffy Pot UK Ltd., Croft Chambers, Croft Road, Crowborough, Sussex. (Peat pots)
Richard Sankey & Son Ltd., The Potteries, Bulwell, Notts. (Plastic pots)
Stewart Plastics Ltd. (Plastic pots and seed trays)
George Ward (Moxley) Ltd., Baggots Bridge, Darlaston, Staffs. (Plastic pots)

## Tubs

Joseph Bentley Ltd. (Wood and plastic)

## Hanging baskets

Calvert Cultivation Ltd., Calvert House, Rickmansworth, Herts
Stewart Plastics Ltd.

## Growing bags

Fisons Ltd., Harston, Cambridge

## Growing bag plant supports

Auriol (Guildford) Ltd., Passfield, Liphook, Hants

## Growing bag capillary trays

ICI Plant Protection

## Composts

John Innes Manufacturers Association, The Horticultural Trades Association, 18 Westcote Road, Reading, Berkshire. (For list of manufacturers who use correct formulae)
J. Arthur Bowers Compost, Lindsey & Kesteven Ltd., Wigford House, Lincoln
Chempak Ltd., Brewhouse Lane, Hertford. (Fertilizer kits for home-made compost and growing bags)
Fisons Ltd. (Levington compost)
Pan Britannica Industries. (Bio compost)
Phostrogen Ltd., Corwen, Clwyd. (Fertilizer kits for home-made compost and growing bags)

## Propagators

George H. Elt Ltd. (Heated by paraffin)
Humex Ltd. (Electrically heated)
Nethergreen Products. (Mist propagation system)

Simplex of Cambridge. (Electrically heated)
George Ward (Moxley) Ltd. (Simple plastic-hooded kind)

## Labels

Joseph Bentley Ltd. (Various)
Clear Span Ltd., Greenfield, Oldham, Lancs. (Anodised aluminium)
Paramount Plastic Products Ltd., Anerley Station Road, London SE20. (With transparent plastic window)
S. H. Rainbow, Summerheath Road, Hailsham, East Sussex. (Plastic)
Synchemicals Ltd., 44/45 Grange Walk, London SE1. (Plastic)

## Seedsmen

Thomas Butcher Ltd., The Garden Centre, 60 Wickham Road, Croydon, Surrey
Samuel Dobie & Son Ltd., Upper Dee Mills, Llangollen, Clwyd
Hurst, Gunson, Cooper, Taber Ltd., Witham, Essex
Suttons Seeds Ltd., Hele Road, Torquay
Thompson & Morgan Ltd., London Road, Ipswich, Suffolk
W. J. Unwin Ltd., Seedsmen, Histon, Cambridge

## Specialist growers

Donald MacLean, Dornock Farm, Crieff, Perthshire. (Wide range of seed potatoes)
Ken Muir, Honeypot Farm, Weeley Heath, Clacton-on-Sea, Essex. (Strawberries and soft fruits)

## Chemicals, fumigants, rooting powders etc

Airwick (UK) Ltd., Brooke House, Church Street, Wilmslow, Cheshire. (Gesal products)
Boots Pure Drug Co. Ltd., Nottingham
Bugges Ltd., Sittingbourne, Kent
Ciba-Geigy (UK) Ltd., Wittlesford, Cambridge
Fumite, Octavius Hunt Ltd., Dove Lane, Redfield, Bristol
Humex Ltd. (Panasand algicide)
ICI Plant Protection
Jeyes (UK) Ltd., Brunel Way, Thetford, Norfolk. (Jeyes' fluid)
May & Baker Ltd., Dagenham, Essex
Murphy Chemical Co. Ltd., Wheathampstead, St Albans, Herts
Nethergreen Products. (Algofen algicide)
Pan Britannica Industries
Synchemicals Ltd. (Wide range including Nippon ant destroyer)

## Fertilizers

Cannock Fertilizers, Cannock, Staffs
Chempak Ltd
Fisons Ltd
ICI Plant Protection
Lindsey & Kesteven Ltd., Wigford House, Lincoln
Maskells Fertilizers, Dirleton Works, Stephenson Street, London E16
Maxicrop Ltd., 21 London Road, Great Shelford, Cambridge. (Based on seaweed)
Pan Britannica Industries
Phostrogen Ltd

## Sprayers

ASL, Plume Street, Birmingham
Tudor Garden Products, Hengoed, Mid Glamorgan, South Wales

## Electric fumigator

Humex Ltd. (Kyldane)

## Various sundries

Joseph Bentley Ltd

# Index

# Index